Vicki —
Female friends are one of
life's greatest treasures and
God's greatest gifts.
Hope you enjoy the book!

Holly Olson

presented to

Vicki

from

Annie

date

May 28, 1997

May our friendship keep growing
and being such a super source
of love, joy and fun!

"*A friend is a present you give yourself.*"

—Robert Louis Stevenson

IN THE COMPANY OF

FRIENDS

Celebrating Women's Enduring Relationships

Brenda Hunter, Ph.D. & Holly Larson

MULTNOMAH BOOKS • SISTERS, OREGON

In the Company of Friends

published by Multnomah Books
a part of the Questar publishing family

International Standard Book Number: 0-88070-889-1

Design by David Carlson

Cover photo by Tamara Reynolds

Printed in the United States of America

Most Scripture quotations are from:
The Holy Bible, New International Version (NIV)
© 1973, 1984 by International Bible Society,
used by permission of Zondervan Publishing House

Also quoted:
The New Revised Standard Version Bible (NRSV)
© 1989 by the Division of Christian Education
of the National Council of the Churches of Christ
in the United States of America

The New King James Version (NKJV)
© 1984 by Thomas Nelson, Inc.

The King James Version (KJV)

For information:
QUESTAR PUBLISHERS, INC.
POST OFFICE BOX 1720
SISTERS, OREGON 97759

96 97 98 99 00 01 02 03 — 10 9 8 7 6 5 4 3 2 1

To all our close friends,

who have been with us in the good times

and the hard times,

who have nurtured us, held us accountable,

and helped us to grow.

—BRENDA & HOLLY

c o n t e n t s

Introduction

Women need other women, cradle to grave. For us, relationships are the essence of life. We almost always put our relationships with our husbands, children, and friends ahead of ambition and material gain. But our fast-paced, time-pressured lives are taking us further and further away from what we value most highly. Who has time anymore for a two-hour lunch or a slow-paced Sunday afternoon with a best friend? Who has time to enjoy soul-searching conversations over endless cups of coffee? When was the last time we were able to drop everything—our commitments, errands, and home responsibilities—for a spontaneous get-together with a friend who makes us feel truly alive?

Many women we interviewed said they long for more time with close friends, time when they aren't exhausted from working, caring for a family, or simply trying to take care of themselves. This book has been written to give voice to that longing, to celebrate the company of other women, and to reaffirm the life-giving potential of our female bonds. We place enormous value on our relationships with our mothers, daughters, sisters, friends; in fact, deepening and strengthening these bonds is a lifelong goal. But many women in their twenties, thirties, and forties also yearn for a different kind of friendship—one not valued in today's society—a relationship with an older woman or mentor who can help them negotiate life's sometimes perilous rapids.

This book looks at these all-important relationships—to validate, explore, and encourage these ties, to give words to our feelings about these passionate and occasionally problematic bonds. We hope that by reading this book you will feel empowered to strengthen your current relationships and to reach out and create new ones.

Finally, a word about us, the authors of *In the Company of Friends*. We are a mother-daughter team, but we are also dear friends. When I first started thinking about writing a sequel to *In the Company of Women*, it was only natural that I ask Holly, my older daughter who says, "Words are my life," to write this book with me. After all, we have collaborated on so many projects, and we both cherish our female friends. Besides, we bring our different perspectives to this book: I, as a psychologist in her fifties; Holly, as an enthusiastic single professional in her late twenties.

So come join us *In the Company of Friends*. We hope these thoughts will touch your heart and give you words to share with your mother, daughters, sisters, mentors, and friends.

—*Brenda Hunter, Ph.D.*

"Real friends are those who, when you've made a fool of yourself, don't feel that you've done a permanent job."

—Erwin T. Randall

Friends: Part Mother, Sister, Saint

"What is a friend? A single soul dwelling in two bodies."

ARISTOTLE

Friends are among life's greatest treasures. What would we have done without friends in adolescence to help us navigate the travails of puberty and deal with our "unreasonable" parents? And what about our failed romances? Who provides emotional rescue when the man of our dreams becomes the stuff of nightmares? In the presence of close friends, we laugh about what drove us crazy just minutes before. We cry without shame, knowing we will be understood.

"Each friend represents a world in us, a world possibly not born until they arrive, and it is only by this meeting that a new world is born."

—Anaïs Nin, French writer and diarist

Who else but a woman listens with sympathetic nods, wraps us up in a woolly afghan, fixes us lunch, bakes our favorite cookies, and makes us a bottomless cup of tea? Our best friends are part mother, sister, saint; they know our souls and love us into our strengths and despite our weaknesses.

—Holly

"I think of my women friends as a raft we make with our arms. We are out there in the middle of some great scary body of water, forearm to forearm, hand to elbow, holding tight. Sometimes I am part of the raft, joining up with the others to provide safe harbor; other times I need to climb aboard myself, until the storms subside and I can see my way clear to swim to shore. The raft drifts apart when it's not needed, but never disbands, never forgets."

—Beverly Lowrey, <u>Self</u> magazine, May 1994

"Few comforts are more alluring for a woman than the rich, intimate territory of women's talk. A woman friend will say, 'You are not alone. I have felt that way, too. This is what happened to me.' *Home*, in other words."

—Elsa Walsh, <u>Washington Post</u> reporter

Women in America today need permission to pursue female relationships. Time spent with our friends is not *wasted* time but vital time when we grow as women. We become soulless if we're driven every minute of the day. When did accomplishments ever keep anybody from being lonely? And when did high salaries ever make us laugh? If we deepen our significant relationships, not only will we shed the blues, but we will feel lifted and renewed. Understood. Ready to tackle the next thing.

"The worst solitude is to be destitute of sincere friendship."

—*Francis Bacon, English philosopher*

"I need to vent. Stop trying to fix things! Let me vent!" So exclaimed Cindy after I had cut her off half a dozen times with suggestions, advice, and exhortation. She had had a rough week: car problems, work problems, friend problems. She wanted to spill her guts, not have me suture them. And so, after laughing at her earnestness, I let her do just that. Too often we forget that the greatest service we can give our friends is a listening ear and an open heart.

—*Holly*

"You meet your friend, your face brightens—you have struck gold."

—*Kassia, ancient philosopher*

One national survey of women—ages seventeen to sixty—concluded that "relationships seem to be the only reliable source of joy for many women."[1] We know that despite life's inevitable ups and downs, we can count on our champions and coaches—our best friends—to dispel the threatening clouds and laugh with us.

Who but another woman understands how it feels to be trapped in a body that's threatening to self-destruct?

Two female coworkers were talking over lunch. One, in her late thirties, was crampy and irritable. "I've got PMS," she groaned, "and I'm having a bad hair day." Her older friend, herself in the throes of postmenopausal estrogen withdrawal, snapped back, "You drive, I'll shoot."

"Oh, the comfort—the inexpressible comfort of feeling safe with a person, having neither to weigh thoughts, nor measure words—but pouring them all out—just as they are—chaff and grain together—certain that a faithful hand will take and sift them—keep what is worth keeping—and with the breath of kindness blow the rest away."

—Dinah Craik

"The moment we laid eyes on each other we knew being friends was going to be the best kind of trouble."

—Pam Tillis on her friendship with Callie Khouri,
screenwriter for Thelma and Louise,
as quoted in Self magazine, May 1994

"Women miss the backyard fence. Even working women. We are community people, and even in the workplace, we attempt to create a sense of community."

> —Heidi Brennan, Director of Public Policy,
> Mothers at Home

Friendship is an art. *Webster's* defines an art as a "skill acquired by experience, study or observation, such as the art of making friends." You can become expert in the art of friendship by acquiring social skills and observing friendship's timeless rituals. Even in "unbirthday" times make your friend feel special by writing her a note, kidnapping her for breakfast at a diner, or cashing in frequent-flier miles for a trip for two. And in the dead of winter, remember her with a bunch of violets, a book, or pâté and French bread for an impromptu winter picnic.

Women who are rich in friendships enjoy better physical health, live longer, and are less prone to alcoholism, suicide, and mental illness than those who are lonely and isolated. If we see our close friends at least every two to three weeks, we can better handle the major stresses of life's transitions: unemployment, divorce, and death of a family member.

> —Adapted from sociologist Pat O'Connor, *Friendships Between Women*

"My friend Cassie and I have been friends for forty-four years," says Jenny. "My house faced hers. My parents called her 'Cassandra Jean the flying machine.' They said that if we were talking on the phone, I wouldn't have hung up before she'd arrive.

"We spent our adolescence walking to Hooks, the local drugstore, talking about what our perfect men would be like, what they'd be wearing, and where we'd meet them—always some foreign country like Cuba. I wore lavender; she, white.

"In the seventh grade we decided to leave New Castle as soon as possible. So when my dad took us to buy school supplies, we bought briefcases.

"When Cassie started her company in '86, she named me as VP on the books. At the time I wasn't in the video business; I was an illustrator. Later I got into advertising and production. When my mother got sick, I flew home, sold her house, and put her in a retirement home. I thought, 'What do I do now?' Cassie called and said, 'Move here. You've been our VP for years.'"

—Jenny, 49, corporate art director

"If you approach each new person you meet in a spirit of adventure, you will find yourself endlessly fascinated by the new channels of thought and experience and personality that you encounter."

—Eleanor Roosevelt

A m y   D a y s

"I've known Amy since kindergarten. She's been my best friend since second grade. Amy taught me long division. We were confirmed at the same time and were attendants at each other's weddings one summer. We went to graduate school and even bought our first houses simultaneously—houses with similar gigantic Los Angeles mortgages.

"Through letters we kept tabs on our hopes and dreams, and when I learned of her pregnancy through a Christmas card, I immediately called to tell her of mine. We'd both been afraid to phone our news—afraid of somehow crushing the other with our good fortune.

"I was due twenty-five days before Amy, committed to natural childbirth the Bradley way. Amy had chosen Lamaze. When she called me on the day before my due date, I said that I was in labor and it was sweet of her to call and check on me. She softly replied that she was calling to announce the birth of her daughter, Rebecca Anne, the day before.

"Emily Catherine was born the following day, making our first children both girls, born two days apart. Emily's christening, an intimate affair including Amy and her tiny family, was scheduled a month later. It was the first time we'd seen each other in over two months. Amy had lost her baby weight. I hadn't. Since Amy had a few months before she had to return to work, she suggested that we get together. I agreed and called the next day. Thus began my 'Amy Days.'

"Amy Days were special. They were canceled only for illness. Weekly, we alternated driving the thirty-two miles in Los Angeles traffic—one-and-a-half hours one way, but it was worth it. On Amy Days the dishes and laundry waited until I returned. I left with a light heart, a full diaper bag, and a smile. I would return exhausted from the drive (about half an hour from home, Emily and I would get stuck in a traffic jam that usually provoked her to cry the rest of the way), but I would be renewed, ready to tackle the next week of mothering.

"We planned outings to the library, buggy rides around our neighborhoods, photo sessions with still and video cameras, and excursions to the mall for makeovers. We designed matching Christmas playsuits, carefully sewing to fit growing babies. But mostly we just played with our children and talked.

"My husband's job has taken us to Austin, Texas, fifteen hundred miles from Amy, but we still stay in touch. Through phone calls, Amy and I have shared the scariness of bronchitis, the trials of potty training, and the joy we have in our blossoming children. And though my Amy Days are now mere phone calls at odd hours, they are no less important to the fabric of my life."

—Lisa Latham Green,
Welcome Home magazine,
January 1996

"Happy is the house that shelters a friend."

—*Ralph Waldo Emerson*

Women, especially if single, need other women as never before. Emancipated from their families, they may come home to empty apartments after working long days in anonymous office high-rises. Who helps them with their lonely feelings? Who comforts them when life gets overwhelming? Their girlfriends, their mothers, or both. As they pick up the phone, they know they will be instantly understood, commiserated with, and encouraged. Could Alexander Graham Bell ever have imagined that he would one day become the patron saint of women's friendships?

"Anyone can sympathize with the sufferings of a friend, but it requires a very fine nature to sympathize with a friend's success."

—*Oscar Wilde*

Women always need other women to come alongside and speak their language: the language of feelings and of the heart. Our conversations with our female friends help shape our attitudes, identities, and vision for the future.

"The greatest thrill about a good friendship is when you're with your friend you don't have to complete all your sentences. She knows what you mean. In that sense it's like a marriage. And the really, really good friends are the ones you can just *be* with. You don't have to worry about what you're going to say next. Remember the scene in *When Harry Met Sally* where Harry says, 'Isn't it nice when you can just sit with someone and not have to talk?'"

—Beth, 32, kindergarten teacher

Women have more—and deeper—friendships than men throughout their lives. Women also disclose more than men, and their friendships are richer in spontaneity and confidences.

—Adapted from sociologist Robert Bell, Worlds of Friendship

Male development is hierarchical, like a pyramid. Throughout their lives men are concerned with ascendancy and self-protection in conversation and life. Female development, on the other hand, is interconnected, like a web. Women disclose, making themselves vulnerable in order to anchor their lives in relationships with men, children, and other women.

—Adapted from psychologist Ruthellen Josselson,
Finding Herself

"A friend loves at all times,

  and kinsfolk are born to share adversity."

                —*Proverbs 17:17, NRSV*

Women are twice as likely to get depressed as men. A major cause? Social isolation. If we have only superficial conversations at work or if we're home alone with small children, we are likely to become depressed. To find our way out, we must begin to build a supportive network of other women that includes friends and mentors. It also helps enormously if we have a warm, affectionate bond with our mother. But if that's not possible, it's important to make peace with her in our heart.

"Girlhood friendships give us a model we keep trying to recreate throughout our lives, of a perfect union with a single solitary other."

           —*Beverly Lowrey, Self magazine, May 1994*

"We cannot tell the precise moment when friendship is formed. As in filling a vessel drop by drop, there is at last a drop which makes it run over; so in a series of kindnesses there is at last one which makes the heart run over."

         —*James Boswell, Scottish lawyer and author*

Our friendships with other women are based on intimacy rather than shared activities. We love to talk, visit, just *be* together. Conversing for hours over a Coke or a cappuccino, while a male waiter goes berserk, satisfies something deep within us. How different for men. While we sit, gazing raptly into another woman's eyes, men look out in the same direction, discussing the worlds of sports, politics, investments. And neither sex envies or understands the conversational world of the other.

"A friend is, as it were, a second self."

—Cicero

Friendship between women thrives when it contains nurturing, even maternal, acts. We especially enjoy small or unexpected gifts that meet an unexpressed need. Picking up the check when your friend is in a financial squeeze, offering to proof a school paper or work presentation, or washing her dustmobile when her life is frantic are all wonderful talismans of devotion and care.

"A friend may well be reckoned the masterpiece of Nature."

—Ralph Waldo Emerson

A *New Woman* survey on friendship found that 85 percent of the women polled had a "soul mate." The surprise? Ninety percent of the time that soul mate was another woman. In fact, most women polled said they communicated better with a female best friend (62 percent) than with a husband (51 percent).[2] Apparently, while husbands give us love, confidence, and support, our female friendships provide us with those easy and open confidences we crave.

Other researchers have found that women who have close friends are happier in their marriages. Let's face it: If we have friends to confide in, we put less pressure on our husbands. We don't "talk them to death," as one newly married husband said.

"Crossroads friends" are important for "what was." In these friendships we shared a crucial, now past, time of life—"a time, perhaps when we roomed in college together; served a stint in the U.S. Air Force together; or worked as eager young singles in Manhattan together; or went through pregnancy, birth and those first difficult years of motherhood together." With these crossroads friends, we have a special, tender intimacy that is dormant, waiting to be periodically revived.

—Taken from Judith Viorst,
Necessary Losses

"Sooner or later you've heard all your best friends have to say. Then comes the tolerance of real love."

—Ned Rorem,
American composer and writer

Six A.M. Two women in windsuits are out for their morning walk. As they walk, they talk about their important relationships: husbands, kids, coworkers. They occasionally touch each other's shoulders, stop, face each other, and laugh. A sun-dried, seventy-something man, wearing a neon orange ski hat, walks by, smiles, and says, "You two look like you're doing ballet together." And so they are. As friends, they are dancing in synchrony: listening, encouraging, challenging each other.

"Fate chooses our relatives, we choose our friends."

—Jacques Delille

The most common characteristic of best friends, according to one national survey on friendship, was intuition. When asked to describe a best friend, the majority of women said, "She reads my mind."[3]

"Do not forsake your friend and the friend of your father,

    and do not go to your brother's house when disaster strikes you—

    better a neighbor nearby than a brother far away."

—Proverbs 27:10

We can't expect our friends to fill us up or to define who we are. Nor should we use our friends as a way of escaping feelings of boredom, emptiness, or self-doubt. To be comfortable with others we must first be comfortable inside our own skin. To be truly *with* others, we must first be *with* ourselves.

"Wounds from a friend can be trusted,

    but an enemy multiplies kisses."

—Proverbs 27:6

When we converse, we get 90 percent of our information from nonverbal cues that we unconsciously assimilate and interpret, and only about 10 percent from the actual spoken words. The point? We'll learn as much—if not more—from our friend's body language, demeanor, facial expressions, and tone of voice as we will from what she says.

To be a good friend I need time alone. Many of my extroverted friends can't understand that I'm perfectly happy, lolling on my sofa in my watermelon-colored living room, reading magazines and books, a shaggy-haired, hygiene-impaired cat snoring at my feet, snacks an arm's length away.

My overachieving pals pack every minute with parties, dinners out, ministry activities, tutoring, morning prayer coffees. They live on the run, overworked, perpetually tired, gray circles creasing their eyes, the stray yogurt accumulating mold in an unused refrigerator, Coke cans rolling across their cars' floor mats.

I can't do that. My condo is my castle. I pad around in gray sweats, take phone calls prone, minister to an army of wrinkled plants, retire happily between flannel sheets, write scintillating thoughts in a collection of odd notebooks. I thrive in solitude. It is then that I am most myself, thinking the stray great thought and thousands of little ones. Only after I have appreciated my own company, am I ready to enter another's.

—Holly

"Friendliness is contagious. The trouble is, many of us wait to catch it from someone else, when we might better be giving them a chance to catch it from us."

—Donald A. Laird

Several years ago a husband called the mental health clinic where I worked, telling the scheduler that his wife needed to see a therapist. (As a therapist I am always leery when one marital partner tries to send the other in for therapy.) "What seems to be the problem?" the scheduler asked.

"She's suffering from mental-pause," replied the man.

When we hit midlife—and experience occasional short-term memory loss or "mental-pause"—that's when we really need the support of our female friends.

—Brenda

Friendship is one of the things women do best. We may not all be tennis champs, CEOs, or caterers to the stars, but most of us are adept at the art of friendship.

Stanford University psychiatrist David Spiegel selected fifty women who were being treated for metastatic breast cancer to participate in weekly support meetings. At the end of a year, these women had experienced 50 percent less pain, were less depressed, and felt more positive than the control group which had received only conventional treatment. Better yet, the support group members survived twice as long. Truly our lives depend on the nurture, empathy, and understanding we get from other women.

—Adapted from Ann Japenga, Health magazine, November/December 1995

"Greater love hath no man than this, that a man lay down his life for his friends."

"I'm a little down. No, really down."

"Why?"

"Well…I shouldn't bother you with it."

"Why not? I thought that's what friends were for."

And slowly the story spills out. My most carefree friend, the one who loves chocolate, red-white-and-blue high tops, her wriggly Labrador, and her husband, lets me see behind the smile. The woman who tries to be bubbly for everyone finally trusts me enough to share rock-bottom confidences. She is moving past playmate into the realm of close friend. Past late-night games and Dick Van Dyke replays, Saturday excursions into SoHo and frequent state-to-state phone calls. Later that week I get a thank-you note. "You always know what to say. Thanks. I needed that," she writes. And I feel honored indeed because it is no trouble at all to share a friend's troubles.

—Zoë, 26, media consultant

"Friendships, like geraniums, bloom in kitchens."

—Blanche H. Geffant, writer

In the Company of Friends

"Life without a friend is death without a witness."

—*George Herbert, English poet*

There are three "fruits of friendship": "someone to confide in, get counsel from, and count on to do for you what you cannot do for yourself."[4]

—*Francis Bacon, English philosopher*

"If you're really rooting for your friend, you'll do more than offer emotional support: you'll confront her and try to get her to confront herself. She's likely to resist and tell you to mind your own business. But if you're a true friend, her life choices are your business."

—*Joshua Halberstam, Self magazine, December 1993*

"Friendship is a category each of us invents. The criteria for admission into my friendship Hall of Fame might not pass muster in yours. In essence, a friend is a friend because we say so. The label is the fact. The astounding thing is, regardless of amorphous definition and a lack of objective criteria, each of us is absolutely certain of what we require in a friend."

—*Letty C. Pogbrebin, Among Friends*

"Two are better than one,

>because they have a good return for their work:

If one falls down, his friend can help him up....

Though one may be overpowered,

>two can defend themselves.

A cord of three strands is not quickly broken."

—Ecclesiastes 4:9–12

"The happiest miser on earth—the man who saves up every friend he can make."

—Robert E. Sherwood, American dramatist

A 1990 Gallup poll on friendship found that one out of four adults longs to have more friends. Yet half of those surveyed admit they don't have enough time to spend with the ones they have! Too often we let unimportant obligations crowd out what really matters—the minutes, hours, and days we spend in our friends' company.

"Female friendships are like no other relationship: unconditional, loving, silly, safe. They are our secret weapon."

—Beverly Lowrey, Self magazine, May 1994

A Friendship to Die For

What would you do for your dearest friend? Most of us envision time together, trips, birthday parties, and occasional help or proof of our true commitment to each other. But what would we do if our loyalty and love were truly tested? Two friends found out how they really felt about each other when it became a life-and-death issue.

In a legendary tale of friendship, Phintias is accused of plotting to overthrow Dionysius, the tyrannical ruler of Syracuse from 407 to 367 B.C. After Phintias is sentenced to die, he asks for permission to go home one last time to put his affairs in order. Dionysius considers this request only because Phintias's friend Damon agrees to take Phintias's place, not only being jailed in his stead but even facing possible execution should Phintias fail to return.

Although Dionysius accepts this barter of one life for another, he thinks Damon is a misguided innocent. How will Damon react, the ruler wonders, when he discovers that Phintias has deserted him, leaving him to die in his place? Will he blame Phintias? Will he beg for mercy?

When the crucial day of the execution finally arrives, as Dionysius has suspected Phintias is nowhere to be found. As the soldiers lead Damon to the courtyard for the public execution, at the last possible moment Phintias suddenly appears. Detained because of an injured horse, he had been terrified he would not make it back in time to stay his friend's execution.

Cynical Dionysius doesn't know what to make of this turn of events. His confusion is compounded when the two friends begin to argue about who should be allowed to die. Damon pleads with the ruler, asking permission to die in Phintias's stead, while his friend begs the ruler to ignore Damon's sacrificial offer. So moved is the ruler by this display of genuine love that he not only pardons Phintias, but asks that he, a man who has never known such depth of friendship, be invited into their inner circle.

Adapted from John M. Reisman,
Anatomy of Friendship

What We Look for in Our Friends

*W*hen we asked women what they looked for in friends, more than once we heard, "This is going to sound like someone I want to date!" accompanied by peals of laughter. The women—married, divorced, single—from twenty-five to forty-nine—responded:

— *"Someone who asks questions, but out of genuine interest, not from a sense of duty."*

— *"Honesty."*

— *"A woman who makes me laugh."*

— *"Common values, beliefs, and commitments; not shared facts, like we both went to Disney World when we were eight years old."*

— *"A soul mate."*

— *"Someone willing to confide in me."*

— *"A sense of fairness and trust; that I'm not going to be taken advantage of."*

— *"The freedom to be at ease with each other; not jealous or possessive of time spent with others."*

— *"Interesting. I don't care if you're the meanest person alive, as long as you're interesting."*

— *"That we're at a similar place in our lives."*

— *"Commitment."*

— *"Women who have something to say, who are multilayered, intriguing."*

— *"A two-way friendship."*

— *"Empathy. I can tell my problems to my husband, but he'll try to give me solutions. I need someone just to listen."*

— *"Someone who helps me focus on what's important."*

Friendships for the Long Haul

*"Some friends play at friendship but a
true friend sticks closer than one's nearest kin."*

PROVERBS 18:24, NRSV

Perhaps you've heard the little rhyme "Make new friends but keep the old / one is silver and the other gold." As we live our lives, we need both the challenge and stimulation that new friends provide and the comfort and ease that only our old friends can give. Without our "old, old friends" we must constantly tell people who we are, that we're worth knowing. But our old friends don't require this song and dance. They were there in grammar school when we wore Coke-bottle glasses and braces. We talked with them for hours about our crushes, first dates, and boyfriends. They were bridesmaids in our wedding, good-heartedly wearing teal taffeta gowns for pictures we now both cringe at. They listened to our thirtysomething struggles with the single life or marriage, career, and family. With our old friends we are most truly ourselves—start to finish. They may lack the most up-to-date details about our busy lives, but it only takes a phone call to catch up. Any questions we had about love and acceptance were answered long, long ago.

If we want to keep our friends, we need to brush up on those difficult words "I'm sorry. Will you forgive me?" Unlike the slogan from the sixties novel *Love Story*, love *does* mean saying we're sorry. Again and again.

No one female friend can be all things to us. As George Santayana said, "Friendship is almost always the union of a part of one mind with a part of another; people are friends in spots."

Birthday parties are special times for the expression of friendship. Why not throw a surprise dinner party for the birthday girl or appear at her house for breakfast on the actual day, with oversized muffins and designer coffee in hand? For friends at work you can plan a pizza party or organize a group lunch out. If you're a mom at home, what about planning a luncheon, inviting friends in for tea, or meeting at a local deli for a kids-free breakfast? Sometimes a major birthday calls for a bit of extravagance. Two friends in their midfifties celebrated their mutual birthdays with a spa day. There they donned white terry robes and slippers and treated themselves to a manicure, pedicure, facial, and makeover.

"Our high-pressured lives give us less time to devote to friends even as we need more friends to help us relax from our high-pressured lives. But we rarely talk about it. We don't go into friendship therapy. We just continue feeling inadequate and believing everyone else must be doing better."

—Letty C. Pogrebin, Among Friends

Friendship is not always about basking in the glow of mutual regard. When a friend goes through marital strife, or she loses a job and her self-confidence plummets, the friendship may feel one-sided. We may grow weary of giving emotional support. Some days we may even feel we're drowning in our friend's neediness. But life is chancy. Who knows when we will need to be on the receiving end of empathy? Since close friendships take time and inevitable sacrifice, we can't be committed to too many people at once. No woman has a limitless supply of time and emotional energy.

If you are married, be careful not to treat your single friends as *less than* simply because they're not romantically involved. Be sensitive to their feelings about marriage and don't constantly harp on yours. Instead, stress your mutual interests, shared history, goals, and dreams.

How do you and your best friend handle "airtime"—the time when one of you gets to hold forth, vent, or monopolize the emotional energy? Do you get your 50 percent? If you do all the work of listening, you may train your friend to be self-absorbed and narcissistic. And you'll leave her presence feeling you haven't been heard, feeling lonely. Healthy relationships possess mutuality.

Aristotle describes three types of friendship: those of utility, pleasure, and virtue. In a friendship of utility, we are interested in what another can do for us. In one of pleasure, we simply enjoy another's company. But in friendships of virtue, we love our friend for her integrity and goodness. According to Aristotle, only friendships of virtue endure.

—*Adapted from John M. Reisman,*
Anatomy of Friendship

Being a good friend requires a lot of soul.

"Caroline and I were associate friends. We both shared a third friend, who died when she was only thirty. That's how Caroline and I became true friends: we inherited each other. When my mother got sick, I came back to Indiana and rented Caroline's weekend cottage. We took courses together at the university, went on long walks, took the boat out on the lake. She worried about her kids; I worried about my mom. She was my strength through my mother's illness."

—*Michelle, 55,*
a university professor

The Friendship Drama

According to author and psychologist Joel Block, in *Friendship: How to Get It, How to Keep It,* the friendships of women unfold over the life cycle like a "friendship drama" with four acts.

Act One: Puberty. As we begin to struggle with emotional and physical changes, we look for a girl to "passionately attach" to—a "first friend." Ah, the tenderness and tenacity of these bonds. "The events and contexts of child-hood—embracing one another with tenderness, walking arm and arm, whisper-ing confidences to one another, sleeping at each other's houses—are cherished memories to many women."

Act Two: Adolescence. Our girlfriends become our favorite companions and conspirators. If we can't be together, we keep in touch by telephone, laugh-ing, whispering, whining for hours at a time.

Act Three: The twenties—the least productive years for close female friendships. Women in their twenties have less desire for female companionship than at any other stage because women are often regarded "less as friends and more as diversions when a husband… [is] unavailable."

Finally comes Act Four: The "transitional thirties." Women return to female friendships in earnest in their early thirties, renewing and deepening old friendships. Women in the workplace reach out to create a sense of community. Moms at home look for the emotional support of others like them. These are the years for linking arms with other women.

Although Block concludes his friendship drama in the third decade, many women discover that their best female friendships occur in midlife and beyond. By their late thirties or early forties, most women have settled into career and/or family life and feel comfortable inside their own skin. Just about the time women become less competitive and more self-accepting, their children begin to leave the nest and their hormones surge. With their feelings of loss and raging hormones, women discover in midlife and beyond that they need their close friends as never before.

"We go from a who-are-you phase to a maybe-you're-nice phase to a show-me-I-can-trust-you phase before something 'clicks' and we really *like* a person."

—*Letty Pogbrebin, Among Friends*

"One only understands the things one tames," said the fox. "Men have no more time to understand anything. They buy things all ready made at the shops. But there is no shop anywhere where one can buy friendship and so men have no friends anymore. If you want a friend, tame me."

—*Antoine de Saint-Exupéry, The Little Prince*

Among our friends, we need key players and second stringers. Key players are those soul mates who share our secrets, provide essential emotional supplies, and help us with life's tough transitions. They may live next door or the next continent over, but they populate our Friendship Hall of Fame.

Second stringers, and this is not meant to be a negative term, are those women who may become best friends. But these newer friendships must still be tested by life: we have yet to go over an emotional Niagara Falls in a barrel together.

Then there is another category of second stringers with whom we share common interests rather than confidences. Writer Judith Viorst calls these "special interest friends." Maybe they're our tennis buddies, our old movie buffs, or fellow Sunday painters. They may tutor inner-city kids with us or attend the same Bible study. "The emphasis in these friendships is on doing rather than being," says Viorst in *Necessary Losses*. We are not necessarily committed to these relationships and may never be. Months can go by without seeing these occasional friends, and neither party feels guilty. Yet when our lives do intersect, we feel the richer for it.

"With every friend I love who has been taken into the brown bosom of the earth a part of me has been buried there; but their contribution to my being of happiness, strength and understanding remains to sustain me in an altered world."

—*Helen Keller*

Pay attention to your friend's body language—eye contact, folded arms, leaning forward or into the chair—and try to hear the unspoken message underneath her words. Is she sad or lonely today? Does she smile and say she's fine but doesn't really mean it? Ask gently probing questions. After you've listened and even mirrored back to her what she has said—so she truly feels heard—only then should you offer advice. If she cries, don't hesitate to comfort her.

"Serendipitous friends" are those women who enter our lives when we're not looking for them. We may not initially be attracted to them because they don't appear similar to us in important ways. Sometimes they're neighbors, office mates, or friends of friends who casually cross our paths.

Sally remembers a neighbor who became a serendipitous friend. At first, Joan's superficiality drove her into a frenzy. Day after day Joan talked about impersonal topics, disclosing little. Sally was ready to pull the plug on this relationship one day when Joan popped over for tea. "God," Sally prayed, as she waited for the water to boil, "I've had it with Joan. She and I can't seem to talk about anything meaningful." As Sally walked back into the living room, teapot in hand, Joan looked up at her and quietly said, "My husband had an affair during our last military posting." Her risky confession opened the door to a candid and rich conversation and, over time, a deep and lasting friendship.

Years ago a dear college friend spoke of close friendships as a Mutual Admiration Society. This phrase aptly describes how I feel about my closest friends and how they respond to me. It's wonderful to draw the best from other people—to motivate and encourage—and to receive their love and praise in kind. With these fringe benefits, I know I'll be a card-carrying member of the Mutual Admiration Society for life.

—Holly

Sometimes a client comes for therapy, complaining about being friendless. As I listen, I often discover that she feels rejected by a parent—usually her mother—and lacks confidence that she is worth knowing. Together we work on changing her attitudes and beliefs about herself—on increasing her self-esteem—and on developing social skills. Along the way I share with her the story Dr. Harville Hendrix tells about a friendless client named Walter, in *Getting the Love You Want*.

"Harville," he said to me as he slumped into the chair, "I feel really terrible. I just don't have any friends."

I was sympathetic with him. "You must be very sad. It's lonely not having any friends."

"Yeah. I can't seem to…I don't know. There are no friends in my life. I keep looking and looking, and I can't seem to find any."

Walter was locked into a view of the world that went something like this: wandering around the world were people on whose forehead were stamped the words "Friends of Walter," and his job was merely to search until he found them.

"Walter," I said with a sigh, "do you understand why you don't have any friends?"

He perked up. "No. Tell me!"

"The reason you don't have any friends is that there aren't any friends out there."

His shoulders slumped.

I was relentless. "That's right," I told him. "There are no friends out there. What you want does not exist." I let him stew in this sad state of affairs for a few seconds. Then I leaned forward in my chair and said, "Walter—listen to me! All people in the world are strangers. If you want a friend, you're going to have to go out and make one!"

—*Brenda*

My friend Jenise has taught me that friendships can ripen with age. She's a veteran of decades-long relationships; I'm working on five- and seven-year bonds. We met on a mountainside, and our lives have taken us over quite a lot of hard climbs since. She has seen me at my worst and fearlessly returns for more.

—*Holly*

Having couple friends over for dinner at least once a month will not only enrich your marriage but will also provide intellectual stimulation. If you work full-time, organize potluck dinners, invite friends over for pizza and old movies, or cook a quick stir-fry.

If you are married and a mother at home, have other mothers and their children in for coffee, lunch, or tea each week. Or you can start a neighborhood moms' support group that meets regularly, organize a mom's co-op, or join a mother and baby swim class. One young mom said, "I try to never miss my daughter's play groups. While she plays, I talk to the other moms. They make me feel normal, that I'm an okay mom."

If you are newly engaged or married, you probably feel you have little need for friends. In fact, studies show that newlyweds have the fewest friends of all. But at some point—after six months or a year—after a three-day blizzard, a basketball playoff, or a romantic movie too many—you and your true love will realize you need to go beyond the cocoon of your relationship and spin webs to connect with friends, both new and old. If you do this, your relationship will be the richer for it. Kahlil Gibran said it well: "Let there be spaces in your togetherness." Space for solitude. Space for same-sex friends and other couples.

A First Lady's First Friend

The morning eighteen-year-old Bess Wallace awakened abruptly to her father's suicide, she chose not to turn to her mother for comfort but to her best friend, Mary Paxton, who lived next door. The two young women walked together for hours as Mary comforted Bess.

Years passed, and Bess met and married a politician who, in 1945, took her to the White House as his partner in the political arena. Bess shared the full range of her husband's emotional and professional interests. According to her daughter Margaret, it was a marriage of equals. "Night after night she and dad met in his upstairs study to discuss the decisions, the controversies, the personalities he faced in a world devastated by the most terrible war in history." And Harry Truman's love and faith helped heal Bess's childhood sorrow.

Although Bess was a famous first lady, she never lost touch with her friend Mary Paxton. They often corresponded, and when Mary's husband and son both died, she turned to Bess for comfort. Even in old age, these two women nurtured their friendship. They kept a steady stream of notes and gifts flowing between them, relishing the comfort and joy of a lifelong friendship.

Adapted from "Faith of a First Lady"
by Margaret Truman
Guideposts, October 1995

Girlfriends are like old blankets. After a hard day, we curl up on the phone with them, feeling warmed in our soul; we clutch these friendships to us when the winds of crisis blow. No matter how tatty with age, we carry our friends with us and never outgrow them.

Once a bond is forged in the fire of intense emotional experience and it endures, we develop those forever friends, whether we see them frequently or seldom. If they live far away, we pick up where we left off when they next enter our lives. We have the ability to suspend dialogue, but not feelings, to love each other despite the distance and the years that separate us.

When a friend is in trouble, she doesn't want you to solve her problem. Instead she wants you to listen with compassion and empathy. She wants to find a pair of warm eyes staring back at her. If she asks for advice, give it. If practical help is appropriate—meals, baby-sitting—extend that, so your friend knows you care. But what's most important to her is the sense that you understand, that she is not alone in her pain.

We need our friends in good times, but we especially need them when life becomes fragile. Yum, a Saks Fifth Avenue hair stylist in Tysons Corner, Virginia, is providing support for her Bombay-based friend Lali, who's just discovered she has cancer.

January 1996

My dear sweet Yum Yum:

Thank you so much for your love and kindness; it was so sweet of you to come to my place and give me a haircut. I really appreciated it. Yum, within a few days of our arrival in Bombay, I was back in the hospital undergoing tests. This time the diagnosis was cancer. Breast cancer in the fourth stage, an advanced stage. It has spread to my lungs. That is why I could not breathe, walk, or talk in Washington, D.C. An operation is not possible, so my only recourse is chemotherapy. I've already had my first dose of chemo; it left my body weak and fragile and made me lose my hair. I have no hair now. I'm bald and sexy. The doctors are afraid to give me a second dose of chemo; they say that my body will not withstand it. So I'm on pills, which does the same work, but is gentler. With the help and love and prayers of family and friends, I am getting better and better every day. Sweet Yum, please pray that I go through this experience with courage, strength, patience, and a smile. The doctor says that if he can stop 60 percent of the cancer, then I will have two to five more years to live. But I think that the Divine Doctor has other plans for me. My family is encouraging me to fight for my life; I think God will help me to do so.

I live one day at a time, not knowing what the future holds. Sweet Yum, please remember that I love and miss you very much. I treasure all the times we spent together and all my beautiful and chic haircuts. I wish you a wonderful 1996. Today is one of my good days and I can sit up longer; I'm glad I got this chance to write to you. I'm very tired now; it's time for me to take my oxygen. Do keep in touch. Love you,

Lali

How Would You Rate Yourself as a Friend?

☐ Do you reach out to others rather than always expect that they will call or come to see you? Do you reciprocate?

☐ When you meet other women, are you open to the possibility that they may become future allies, confidantes, best friends?

☐ Do you approach others with an attitude of acceptance and interest?

☐ Are you a good listener, or do you claim more than your share of the airtime?

☐ Do you refuse to become the only nurturer in the relationship?

☐ Are you loyal, and do you guard your friends' secrets?

☐ Do you practice unsolicited acts of kindness?

☐ Do you live an authentic life based on your values and beliefs?

☐ Can you ask for and grant forgiveness?

☐ Can you listen when a friend tells you that you've hurt her, or do you withdraw or get defensive?

☐ Do you encourage other people to develop their strengths and graciously help them overcome weaknesses?

☐ Can you enjoy a friend's good fortune— whether in marriage, motherhood, or career— even if you aren't on a parallel track?

Refusing to Dance Away

"Friendship is like money, easier made than kept."

SAMUEL BUTLER, ENGLISH WRITER

How do you handle conflict with a friend? According to a 1990 Gallup survey, most Americans avoid clashes with their friends. When asked, "Do you ever get into serious arguments with your friends?" only 13 percent said yes. That means a lot of us walk around, suppressing our hurt or angry feelings, afraid we will lose our friend if we confront her. Unfortunately unresolved anger doesn't just disappear. And hurt feelings don't simply evaporate. They often resurface as migraines, muscle tension, or stomachaches, and inevitably create psychological distance. When we interviewed other women, we found the majority stuff their negative feelings while a few work through them:

The Avoider. "I let things go until they're overwhelming. Then I become very unhappy. I'll either avoid the issue completely or subconsciously create a situation to bring the issue up. In the meantime I tell myself it doesn't matter, that the relationship isn't that important to me, but in my heart it is."

—*Penny, 29, corporate professional*

The Problem-Solver. "If you don't deal with conflict, your friendships die from the inside out."

—*Danni, 35, communications director*

"Conflict usually arises because of a misunderstanding. So I talk through it. I make sure my friend understands that if it was my fault, it wasn't intentional. And if she hurts me, then I'm comfortable telling my best friend and waiting to hear her explanation."

—Carrie, 25, program coordinator

The Stuffer. "I'll go off into a corner, get quiet, and pout, then come back, but never acknowledge that I'm hurt. I act as if everything's normal. I tell myself that I don't hold it against them, but at some level I do. I see the problem as a limitation and avoid similar situations. I don't want to be disappointed twice by the same thing. When I've been involved in confrontations, every time the friend has come to me."

—Julia, 25, corporate educator

The Disappearer. "I evaporate when there's conflict. My best friend gets over it quickly; I don't. The way we talk about it is to joke about it later. It's acknowledged in a number of little ways, but it's never fully resolved."

—Liz, 47, musician

When a friend hurts or ignores us, we begin an inner dialogue. Exonerating ourselves, we devalue our friend. We tell ourselves how wronged we were and how insensitive she is. After all, can't she see how right we are? The longer we refuse to address the breach between us, the more we dwell on the problem and withdraw. To reconcile, we need to relinquish any self-righteousness and own our mistakes.

Linda LeSourd Lader, mother of two darling girls and cofounder of the annual Renaissance gathering in Hilton Head, South Carolina, says that she learned to deal with conflict in her twenties when she lived in Washington, D.C. with two other women. "That's when I developed friendships where there was a real commitment to each other and when we said there would be no 'back door' in our friendships. If you lock the door in a friendship, you know you can't run from your problems and misunderstandings; you have to find a way to work them out. How can we expect to hang in there and keep our marital commitments if we haven't had any prior practice with our committed female friendships?"

"To let friendship die away by negligence and silence is certainly not wise. It is voluntarily to throw away one of the greatest comforts of this weary pilgrimage."

—*Samuel Johnson, English writer*

I have just come from the company of friends. For several hours this morning four of us—women of a certain age—huddled in a restaurant booth, sharing our needs, concerns, unanswered questions. Our hearts. Two of us cried after deep confessionals; all of us laughed. The waiter must have thought we were nuts as we sat there, laughing through our tears. But that's the way we women are. We cry in front of our truest friends, assured we're in a safe place, and sometimes we laugh through our tears.

—Brenda

While no female friendship is completely without rivalry, most can handle that tension openly and with humor, as did two women walking to their cars one day after lunch. Both looked at the emerald green, brand-new Jaguar and the faded, ten-year-old Chevy with a dented fender, parked side by side. Then the owner of the Chevy turned to her friend and said, "Now, honestly, which one of us do you think God loves the best?"

"It is well, when one is judging a friend, to remember that he is judging you with the same godlike and superior impartiality."

—Arnold Bennett, English novelist

I used to be a flamethrower in my friendships. A friend would hurt me, and pfiss! A verbal torch would come whizzing her way. Imagine my friend's surprise when she realized she risked incineration after making an innocent mistake! I learned the hard way—by almost losing an important friendship—that this was not an appropriate way to deal with hurt and angry feelings. I've learned by talking things over with my best friend that problems can be discussed rationally and without ire. I've also learned that people have different perspectives; sometimes there is no easy solution, and you just suck it up and go on.

—Holly

Although women are the world's intimacy experts, many "end their relationships without warning or 'drift away.'" Often women want "peaceable relationships" they can idealize. Apparently many women think of friendship as a "pure" relationship that can't be worked on. Why do we feel this way? We quarrel with family members, husbands, and boyfriends and often resolve our problems. Why can't we do the same with our female friends? Sadly, "the voluntary nature of friendship—the very thing that makes it special—also makes it easier for partners to exit."

—Adapted from Sherryl Kleinman,
Social Forces, March 1989

"If it's very painful for you to criticize your friends, you're safe in doing it. But if you take the slightest pleasure in it, that's the time to hold your tongue."

—Alice Duer Miller

When relationships flounder, they contain two main toxins: blame and choking dependency. Blame always drives people apart. No one enjoys being attacked. So if you're a blamer, it's important to assume responsibility for your feelings and look at what part you play in the problem.

The second toxin—choking, clinging dependency—poisons any relationship. The dependent, insecure person tries to control others by "bleeding the life out of them." This never works. If we are too dependent, other people will sense our neediness and flee. We need to recover our lost strength by confronting our low self-esteem. Only as we learn to love and accept ourselves will we be able to have healthier relationships.

—Adapted from psychologist Joel Block,
Friendship: How to Give It, How to Get It

The freedom to make and break friendships is "at once so seductive and so anxiety-provoking.... If we can be chosen, we can also be 'unchosen.'"

—Lillian B. Rubin, Just Friends

Author Dee Brestin tells the story of Lynn, who anxiously awaited news of her boyfriend, Craig, the pilot of a missing emergency medical helicopter. Finally the call came and it was the worst of all possible news: Craig had died in the crash. Lynn then called her best friend, Susy, who asked Lynn if she wanted her to come.

"'No,' I told her. 'It's not necessary—I'll be OK.' Susy lived so far away; I didn't realize how desperately I would need her when the shock wore off. Thank God she came.

"...I also told my friend Deb to go on home after the helicopter was reported missing. She had worked a long shift and I hated to make her stay—I knew it could be a long, long time. But she stayed all night. She was with me in the morning, when they told me they found the bodies. She cried with me and held me. I'll never forget that."

—*Dee Brestin, The Friendships of Women*

"A true apology is more than just acknowledgment of a mistake. It's recognition that something you have said or done has damaged a relationship—and that you *care* enough about that relationship to want it repaired and restored."

—*Norman Vincent Peale*

"True friendship is never serene."

—*Marquise de Sévigné, French writer*

What predicts how we handle conflict in our close relationships? Our relationships with Mom and Dad. Those of us who felt secure in our parents' love and affection are more assertive in dealing with conflict than those who did not. And we tend to have fewer conflicts in our friendships and romantic attachments generally. Anchored in our parents' love, we are less touchy or supersensitive. This not only enables us to risk honesty but to choose healthier friends in the first place.

"Any close relationship, whether with a mate or a friend, has the potential to recreate within us some of the same feelings of rivalry we had with a sibling, the same separation struggle we engaged in with a parent, the same dependency needs, the same vulnerability, the same conflicts, the same ambivalence."

—Lillian B. Rubin, *Just Friends*

What are the benefits of resolving conflicts in our important relationships? If we're successful, our friendships become deeper, richer, happier. We may become forever friends. By refusing to run away and instead learning to speak the truth in love, we become anchors to each other in a sometimes chaotic world. As we hone our communication skills, we discover an unexpected benefit. We have grown more confident in our relationships with *all* other women, including our mother, sisters, and daughters.

What Helps When Hard Times Come

When you have conflict with a friend, you need to be willing to take the initiative to bring light and reconciliation. Even if you're fearful of rejection, go to your friend and say, "Something has happened to our friendship. I feel a distance. Can we talk about it?" You may have to overcome your pride, but what comfort is pride if you lose a dear friend?

When you are together, it's best to focus on goals that are larger than any personal differences. You can begin by saying, "Your friendship means the world to me. We've shared so much. And you probably feel just as hurt as I do. Can we talk about what's going on—our positive and negative feelings, while remembering that our friendship is big enough to survive this?" Once the conversation begins and the heat and the tears come, try to stay on track. If you feel overwhelmed by your friend's emotional intensity, talk to yourself, stay calm, count to ten, and then mirror back all that she's said. Use her words, asking her, "Is this right? Is this how you feel?" Keep doing this until she lets you know that she feels she has been heard and that you truly understand her perspective.

After you've mirrored and affirmed your friend's feelings, empathize. Imagine how it feels to be *her* in this relationship. After all, she has her own perspective, and the intensity of her feelings reveals her underlying hurt. Only when you've genuinely sympathized with her is it time to share your perceptions. Once she feels she has been heard and understood, she will be better able to listen. A word of warning: your friend will get angry if she feels you haven't truly listened but have simply waited impatiently for your turn to recite your litany of complaints. It's important to listen with your eyes, ears, heart. Only then have you earned the right to speak.

As you tell your side of the story, share your perceptions, your hurt feelings. Hopefully, your friend has the skills to listen to you as attentively as you've listened to her. If she does, you will have the wonderful feeling of being heard and understood. You may be surprised at the intensity of your emotions because you may have had few, if any, who listened to your heart. Don't be afraid to cry. Most women have that marvelous ability to experience relief and healing once tears start to flow.

After you sense your friend's understanding, it helps to say you're sorry and ask her to forgive you. If she will, you've kept a friend. If she asks for forgiveness too, it will be easier to accept her back into your heart without reservations. To maintain a close relationship each needs to be willing to ask for and grant forgiveness. And if your friend can't bring herself to do this? Then tell her this hurts and see if she can overcome her pride.

Finally, talk briefly about how to avoid a breach in the future. Set some ground rules. Agree not to make negative assumptions or impugn each other's motives. Avoid the blame game. Keep heat to a minimum, speak rationally, and avoid accusations. By setting boundaries and dealing with problems and hurt feelings as they arise, you will not only maintain but deepen your friendships with other women.

"It appears that genuine friendship cannot possibly exist where one of the parties is unwilling to hear the truth and the other equally indisposed to speak it."

—Cicero

The most frequent cause of the death of women's friendships is betrayal. We can put up with a lot of petty selfishness and thoughtlessness, and we feel sad when friends move away and seldom call, but we cannot easily stomach betrayal. That dagger pierces our hearts too keenly.

Did you know that research has found the end of female friendships more painful than the demise of romantic love? People commiserate when a woman loses a boyfriend, but nobody "rushes around with a hot dinner or evening entertainment when a best girlfriend is lost." Consequently, the loss of an important female friend leaves us "temporarily fragile. We want to be cared for, but at the same time we're afraid we'll be judged harshly for having needs."

Adapted from Susie Orbach and Luise Eichenbain,
Bittersweet: Facing Up to Feelings of Love,
Envy and Competition in Women's Friendships

What if a friendship ends? Sadly, some do. It may help to know there are identifiable stages in the dissolution of relationships, beginning with unhappiness with a partner, confronting the partner, telling others about the relationship distress, and finally the "grave dressing stage"—burying the friendship and going on. Repair is possible at each stage if *both* partners desire it. But in friendship, as in marriage, it is not enough for only one party to want the relationship to continue. Both have to become reinvested in the relationship, and even then, hard work and fits and starts lie ahead.

—*Adapted from Steve Duck,* Repairing Personal Relationships

I tease one of my dearest friends by saying that she and I have taken graduate courses in conflict resolution. Although we laugh, we agree that early on we had our fair share of arguments. Wounded in earlier friendships, it took us time to learn to trust each other. Fortunately, along the way we agreed to turn down the volume and speak to each other with kindness and tact. Always we try to defuse situations with laughter. But should all else fail, we leave messages on each other's answering machines to ponder before our next meeting. Ah, the wisdom that finally comes in one's fifties!

—*Brenda*

"But if the while I think on thee, dear friend,

All losses are restor'd and sorrows end."

—*William Shakespeare*

I will long remember when my friend Ros taught me that friendship could not only handle conflict but grow deeper in the process. One day I became angry at Ros but was afraid to tell her. At that time I lived in London with my young daughters, recovering from a failed marriage. Since my first husband had walked away from our seven-year relationship, I couldn't believe a mere friendship could endure conflict. A therapist, Ros addressed my hurt and angry feelings. Once we had dealt with the problem, she said something that caught me completely off-guard: "I am your friend for life." While I didn't believe her then—I was too wounded to trust anybody at that point—the past twenty-five years have proven her true. Still close friends, we frequently make transatlantic calls just to keep in touch. And we visit each other every year or two. We are well along in our friendship for life.

—*Brenda*

When a close friendship ends, we grieve. Sometimes we get angry. We may confide in another friend, a husband, or our mother. We may go to God and tell him how hurt we feel. But then we need to take a long, hard look at the friendship. How much responsibility for the death of the relationship is ours? Of course, it's tough to be honest with ourselves, but some soul surgery is necessary. Only as we see our human foibles as well as our friend's will we grow, letting go forever of our fantasy of the perfect friendship. And someday—in another friendship perhaps—we may find that we have become a better friend—wiser, less demanding, more sensitive.

Mothers and Daughters: First Friends

We will hear our mother's voice in our head
and our heart as long as we live.

I am passionate when it comes to my daughters. In an era when career is glorified and children's needs minimized, rearing my two daughters has been the most challenging and rewarding work I've ever done. Any other accomplishment pales in comparison.

My love affair with my children began before they were born. In fact, I used to tease them by saying I had known them from the womb. "Gag me, Mom!" was usually the response when they were in junior high. I was amused. They didn't understand that as a teenager I didn't even particularly like children and that later I had children, in part, because in the sixties it was the expected thing for a young married woman to do.

But my daughters—with their love, demands, and occasional surliness—have changed me forever. And I am the better for it.

—Brenda

A child's relationship with his mother is "unique, without parallel, established unalterably for a whole lifetime as the first and strongest love object and as the prototype of all later love relationships for both sexes."

—Sigmund Freud, Outline of Psychoanalysis

Mother, Our First Connection

What is this thing called mother love that is so powerful and life enhancing? Even before we are able to see her, we come to recognize her voice in the confines of the womb. A French obstetrician who inserted a hydrophone into a woman's uterus as she was giving birth "heard a virtual orchestra of sounds: the mother's loud, thumping heartbeat, all sorts of whooshing and gurgling, the faint voices of the mother and her doctor talking, and in the background, the unmistakable strains of Beethoven's Fifth Symphony."

After birth, we begin to focus on our mother's face. In fact, scientists have found that babies only one minute old will turn their heads 180 degrees to look at a picture of a human face—whether "real or sketched, in the flesh or on film, two- or three-dimensional, even a mask with two eye-like dots." But in time not just any face will do. We prefer our mother's above all the rest. As for voices, studies show that while newborns love the sound of all human voices, they love their mother's best.

We were born, then, programmed to fall in love with our mother. As babies we resonated to her smile; we picked up on her moods; we responded to her with our coos. If we were fortunate, she listened, held us close, cooed back, and established eye contact again and again. We then began a lovely duet with our mother that lasts into adulthood, as long, in fact, as we both have reason and life.

—Adapted from Evelyn Thoman and Sue Browder,
Born Dancing

The Thursday night before my daughter Kristen's wedding I couldn't sleep. I got out of bed, left my snoring husband, and pulled the door shut behind me. Moments later, I gently pushed open her bedroom door and heard her quietly call out to me, "Mom, is that you?"

"I can't sleep."

"I can't either," she said.

So just as I had done many nights when she was a little girl, I lay down on my daughter's bed beside her and stroked her hair. During her childhood, Kris had loved this daily bedtime ritual when, in the dark, she could relax and pour out her heart.

"Mom, I'm anxious," she said.

"About sex?" I asked.

"No, I'm worried about sharing toothpaste. About sharing personal space."

I laughed, enjoying her response. And then my mind shifted gears. "Do you remember when you were four years old and we lived in England? I can still see you with your navy plaid jumper, your blue tights covering your chubby little legs, and those black Mary Jane's. Your hair was so fine; I kept it short and it looked like chicken feathers."

"Yeah, I remember skipping down the street, holding your hand on those mornings after we had taken Holly to school."

And we were off, tripping down memory lane, wrapping up the first twenty-five years of my younger daughter's life, our sleepy voices going back and forth in the dark.

Soon I got up to leave. As I opened the door, I turned and spoke into the silky darkness, "You'll be a beautiful, regal bride in just two days, Krissy, but you'll always be my baby."

—*Brenda*

The power of a mother's love and presence can hardly be overstated. In that vulnerable first year of life, but particularly between six and twelve months, we forge an attachment first to our mother and then to our father that shapes our self-esteem, feelings of personal power, capacity for intimacy, and expectations about how others will respond to us.[1] What our mother and father give us—that legacy of love or pain—will help or haunt us for the rest of our lives.

We encourage separateness, exploration, and autonomy in our sons while maintaining closer ties with our daughters. Even in infancy we encourage our sons to wander further from us than our daughters. Since this is the case, as mothers we need to remember that our daughters will always tend to stay close. Hence, we can enjoy their company while encouraging them to spread their wings.

Mother in the Mirror

Whether we adore her without reservations, or have significant caveats to our affection, we feel passionately about our mothers:

"My mother was always there and always will be. She has unconditionally loved all of us kids. She has reminded me—with tender and compassionate words—when I was in the middle of a terrible time, that God was there and he loved me.

"I fractured my skull when I was in the third grade after convincing my friend to ride me home on her bike. My doctors thought I would go into a coma. My mom came in every morning with a big bag of birthday and sympathy presents. She read the *Prince and the Pauper* to me although I was unconscious for a day and a half. When I came to, I couldn't see. I screamed for her; I wanted *only* her. She stayed all day every day, and my dad came in the evenings.

"Being my mother's daughter is the biggest blessing of my life. You can't put a value on it. I wouldn't trade my parents for any amount of money in the world."

—*Monica, 31, a policy director*

"I love my mom! She always tells me I'm a wonderful surprise: she didn't expect me to turn out this well. I'll never stop looking to her for approval. I don't think a daughter ever does."

—*Barb, 27, foundation executive*

Our relationship with our mother is a defining relationship. She is our mirror. As little girls, we copied her voice, adopted her mannerisms and friendship styles, mimicked her makeup and walk, dressed up in her clothes, and in the process, learned what it was to be female. As she nurtured us, so we are likely to nurture our children.

"Happy children do not ask why their mothers or anybody else loves them; they merely accept it as a fact of existence. It is those who have received less than their early due of love who are surprised that anyone should be fond of them, and who seek for explanation of the love that more fortunate children take for granted."

—Anthony Storr, psychoanalyst

"Can I have your mother?" is a request I sometimes get from friends less fortunate than I. They've heard all about her—the hours we spend yakking in the living room, discussing future life plans, relationships, our feelings, the frequent phone calls. "I just wanted to talk to you," she says sounding girlish and guilty. The spontaneous get-togethers over tea and chocolate chip cookies at our favorite cafe. They marvel that she used to kidnap my sister and me for shopping and lunch out every spring on a school day. I know what I have, and they know what they're missing. "You can borrow her," I say, "but only for a little while. She's mine."

—Holly

A Lesson for Allison

"I am not the kind of guy who normally takes part in feminist 'consciousness-raising' efforts. But I am participating in Take Your Daughter to Work Day today because I have an eight-year-old daughter whose self-esteem matters a great deal to me.

"For the uninitiated, Take Your Daughter to Work Day is an annual event dreamed up by the Ms. Foundation in response to research showing that girls' self-esteem often plummets during the fragile pre-teen and early adolescent years. By exposing young girls to successful women in the workplace, organizers hope that girls will learn to think more highly of females in general and of themselves in particular.

"I have a great day planned for my daughter, Allison. This morning, I plan to take her by the offices of two women whose job it is to meet regularly with members of Congress and other public officials. Then, I plan to have her talk with a young woman who just finished graduate school at Johns Hopkins University and is now serving as a health policy analyst. At lunch, she'll chat with a woman who does some public speaking, and another who crunches numbers in our accounting department. Finally, in the late afternoon, Allison is scheduled to meet with a woman who used to practice law and now manages a bevy of staff writers.

"I am sure all of this will be interesting to Allison. But the time I am most looking forward to is the ride home. For it is then that I plan to point out to my daughter that some of the exciting tasks carried out by my female colleagues in the workplace are tasks my wife performed in jobs she held prior to motherhood. She used to meet regularly with congressmen and senators. She used to do some writing and public speaking. And she has a Phi Beta Kappa key from her college days.

"After I remind my daughter of these things, I plan to turn to her and look her in the eye and say, 'Allison, you must be a very special young girl. Your mother could be using her talents and skills in all sorts of jobs in the workplace, but she has chosen instead to use them at home teaching you. She must love you very, very much and think you are very, very important.'

"Somehow, I think that at that moment my daughter's self-esteem will rise to a level heretofore unimagined by the organizers of Take Your Daughter to Work Day. And for that I owe a debt of gratitude to my wife, whose esteem-building job as a mother at home rarely receives the public esteem it deserves."

—*William Mattox, Vice President,*

Family Research Council

<u>*Wall Street Journal,*</u> *28 April 1994*

If a girl's relationship to her mother is secure and strong. She grows up feeling she can control the good things of her life. She calls; her mother comes. She is hurt; her mother speaks soothing words of comfort. She gets an award at school, and she and her mother dance around the kitchen. The loved daughter develops a sense of personal efficacy and power. Her mother is her cheerleader, confidante, and, eventually, friend.

"Though Mom didn't give us a high standard of living, she gave us a high standard of life. It didn't matter how many rooms our little migrant house had. What mattered was what went on in those rooms."

—Linda Weber, Mom, You're Incredible

Why do our mothers have such power in our lives? For one thing, we share the same sex. According to writer Nancy Chodorow, males pull away from their mothers at an early age and begin to identify with their fathers.[2] But a daughter's development is different. Psychologist Ruthellen Josselson says that a daughter identifies with the first person she loves. "Attachment implies sameness. 'I love my mother and want to grow up to be just like her' is the hallmark of the identification processes in the little girl. With becoming like mother and therefore pleasing her comes the assurance of remaining forever attached to her."[3]

I call my mother "The Southern Princess" with mixed love and exasperation. We may share the same gene pool, but we're on different sides of the high dive. How could the princess, a woman who lacquers on lipstick just to vacuum, have given birth to a girl more comfortable in overalls and high tops? And so the battle begins, a good-natured one, but a struggle nonetheless. "Oh, Holly, you look so beautiful when you put on lipstick," she beseeches. If ignored, the princess becomes more strident. "I will not go shopping with you until you brush your hair!" I love this woman, Revlon's best customer, but the battle of the brushes is far from over. It's beauty queen vs. granola girl, match point.

—Holly

Nobody appreciates mothers more than their single daughters. When asked to name the one person who loved them most and knew them intimately, single women invariably named their mothers.

—Adapted from Carin Rubenstein.
New Woman. October 1993

"When I stopped seeing my mother with the eyes of a child, I saw the woman who helped give birth to myself."

—Nancy Friday. My Mother/Myself

Our mother was our "secure base" as children. She was our touchstone as we, in the heyday of toddlerdom, explored our surroundings. First, the living room. Then the world. When we were young and became frightened, we ran to the shelter of her arms. Over time, we gained confidence that help would always be there when we needed it. Even when our mother grows old and frail, we will still feel that if life is too much with us, we can run home to her for a few days or hours. And her presence will soothe and comfort us just as it did when we were little girls.

Phyllis, an opera singer, grew up on an Iowa farm with her sister and two parents who openly loved each other and their children. "Even when my mother grew feeble in her eighties, long after my father had died and she had left the farm for town, I always felt I could go home if I needed to. I know this sounds crazy—after all, my mother was old—but she personalized 'home' to me."

One gift that comes from a secure relationship with our mother is the gift of intimacy—a gift we will share later with our husbands, children, and close friends. Having been close to our mother since infancy, we do not erect walls for others to scale, as do our insecure counterparts. Nor do we engage in push-pull behavior. Instead, intimacy feels natural, so natural, in fact, we may take it for granted.

"I stood in the hospital corridor the night after she was born. Through a window I could see all the small, crying newborn infants and somewhere among them slept the one who would become mine. I stood there for hours filled with happiness until the night nurse sent me to bed."

—*Liv Ullman*

Who but your mother shares your moments of glory? Who else sees you at your weakest and most vulnerable and picks you up, helping you grow strong? Your mom believes in your dreams, even when they lie in tatters at your feet. She picks you up and helps you dream again.

I spoke at a women's retreat last fall about making peace with mom and turning her into a friend. After the first session, a woman came up to me and said, "I didn't want to come to this conference because I've never felt close to my mother. But after you spoke, I decided to risk something. So I called mom and praised her for the good things she did when I was growing up. I temporarily forgot the deficits. You know, it's the half-full cup or the half-empty one. When I finished, Mom told me how much she loved me and that she was proud of me." Softly crying, this woman then said, "I'm thirty-five years old, and I had never heard my mom say those words."

—*Brenda*

Conducting a New Life

"I can clearly remember sitting on the edge of my bed holding my new baby. We had just gotten home from the hospital, and my husband had left to pick up my mother at the airport. I had a tremendous need for her—not just because I suddenly felt helpless. Rather I was beginning to conduct my own motherhood symphony. I needed my composer to reassure me and remind me in case I forgot the music.

"I am very close to my mom, but much of what I experience as our warm, emotional intimacy and easy rapport is not usually visible to others. We live on opposite sides of the country, exchanging phone calls every two weeks. Yet I have a daily relationship with her by reliving childhood memories.

"These memories are the foundation for how I nurture my children. I enjoy listening to classical music, especially ballet. As my own children spin around to the *Nutcracker Suite*, I recall my mother leaping and spinning through our living room, drawing me into her dance and joy of life.

"My children love it when I turn their stuffed toys into puppets, speaking to them in funny voices. As I do this, I can hear my mother's vocal intonations and sense of humor in my own voice. Instantly, I feel a rapport with her, uninterrupted by time or distance.

"My mother would spontaneously sit down with crayons and paper to draw pictures with me. She was not so much teaching me to draw, but relating to me through that medium—and, in that process, teaching me to love and express myself freely.

"My mother could not afford to buy me lessons in dance, drama, art, and other such unique opportunities. Instead, she nurtured me and my siblings in her own artistic ways. Dance, drama, and art were some of the media she used for communicating her love to us and creating emotional security within us.

"While parents today seem to worry about giving their children enough outlets to help them build self-esteem, the personal lessons I draw from my mother's gifts to me accent what I believe my children need most—the daily creation of spiritual and emotional avenues for communication between us. It is through these that I teach my children. As I do, my mother's presence is not just close by, it is inside me."

—Heidi Brennan,
mother of five

As a doctoral student at Georgetown University, I interviewed over a hundred women suddenly lost in the emotional swamp of first-time motherhood. As I gingerly pushed open hospital room doors, I discovered women of different shapes, sizes, ages, and races. All had one thing in common: they had been captured by their babies. Sometimes they were surprised by the rush of emotion they felt. Not a few cried as they spoke of longing to protect their vulnerable, newly arrived sons and daughters. And most found themselves thinking about their mothers more than they had for years. Said one, "I had no idea that having a baby would make me want my mom by my side. Now we have more in common than we've ever had. I'm a new mother, but I need my mom to mother me."

—Brenda

"My mother takes great pride in her accomplishments, including her children. Our success and happiness are her major concerns. If we aren't experiencing both simultaneously, she takes action. Mother has often gone where angels fear to tread. She loves with passion and practicality, but without intimacy. She blesses and she wounds. She is good and she is sinful. She is wise and she is foolish. As I reached these revelations in my early forties, I also realized that I could never hope to change her. I could only change myself if I wanted our relationship to be different. And so I did.

"This has not been easy. Every inch has been contested. I know at times I hurt my mother deeply as she resists new patterns of relating. But through it all we are learning to respect each other. Sometimes she actually seems relieved to be confronted! At times I still long to crawl into her lap and be held like I never was as a child. Though that time has passed, I can accept and forgive my mother. While we still argue and fail miserably at our attempts to love each other, we can also spontaneously hug each other. This is a new and wonderful thing!

"While the old adage says that mothers 'cut the apron strings,' I believe that sometimes daughters must take up that task."

—*Karen Henry, 43, stockbroker*

"I remember as a small child the sense of power I felt with my mother," says Sabrina, a twenty-seven-year-old consultant. "I used to play a little song on my xylophone. 'I love my Mommy. I love my Mommy.' She would come from any corner of the house, scoop me up, and plant a wet kiss on my cheek.

"When I went to college, I still called Mom almost daily, this time via Bell Atlantic, and we developed a wonderful friendship. Once when I told her that I had a high fever and stiff neck, Mom hung up the phone immediately and drove like a mad woman for several hours to bring me home and play nurse.

"It has given me an incredible sense of security to know that as long as my mother lives—as long as she has her health—she will come when I call. How has that affected me? I can take risks. Best of all, I can trust. Others, God, life. My mom taught me to enjoy the moment and believe that good things will come to me."

Friends tell my daughters that they share some of my mannerisms and we all smile alike. A relative told Holly at a family reunion, "You look just like your mother did at your age, only you're better looking." He was tactless, but accurate. Not only do my daughters share some of my physical traits—Holly is the third generation of Morrison women with pancake-flat feet, and Kris, like me, has brown eyes—but each daughter also shares some of my interests. Kris majored in psychology at college, while Holly, an English major, has become a corporate writer. Each girl, though very much herself, has identified to some extent with me. How do I feel about this? Enormously gratified. I have tried to be there for them, emotionally and physically, and the fact that they have become close friends gives me great joy.

—*Brenda*

As mothers, we invariably see ourselves in our daughters. But we must be careful not to project our unfulfilled hopes and dreams onto them. After all, they are separate beings with highly individualized perceptions and gifts. While we need to urge them to excel, to live good and moral lives, to be generous and compassionate women, our task is to help them dream their own dreams. As our daughters graduate to adult-friend status, perhaps we need to dust off our dreams as well and found our own company, go back to school, or jump-start a career.

"I always had a hard time waking up as a child," says Anne Marie, a sunny forty-three-year-old. "So my mother came into my room each morning with a warm cup of milk laced with coffee and a piece of toast. Gently, she awakened me. Then she would sit down and talk to me for a few moments as I gradually woke up. She did this all the years I was at home. As an adult, I've come to understand just what a sensitive gift this was.

"Later in high school my friends often drove me home, and as I walked up the sidewalk I could hear my mother playing our old piano. I can remember feeling quite happy that she would be home to ask me about my day.

"Mom was a great communicator who talked openly to me about sex. I knew there was this *thing* between her and my father. They loved each other and were strongly attracted to each other sexually. Once when an uncle criticized Mom for her less-than-squeaky-clean house, she told me conspiratorially, 'It's not a clean house that brings your father home.' Because of all my mother gave me, I am able to nurture my children, husband, and friends easily. Friends tease me, saying, 'If you could put that nurture in a bottle and sell it, you'd make a fortune.' I always took this for granted until one day a friend told me I was a rich woman indeed. Since then, I've come to see more clearly the legacy Mom gave me."

—Anne Marie McMichael,
mother of three

My Mother's Lap

"When I was a child, my mother's lap was the warmest and safest place in the world. On my mother's lap, all the troubles of childhood would fade away, and I would be perfectly secure and content.

"I remember simply sitting on her lap for long periods of time. I suspect she had dishes to do, clothes to wash, errands to run, and yet, I sat. But I do not recall her ever telling me she had something to tend to. In fact, it was always I who ventured off first. Perhaps I had finally awakened from sleep, or my childhood hurts had been comforted away, but when I was emotionally full, I got up.

"My mother had two children younger than I, so how was she able to provide this precious gift of time? I wondered this yesterday, when my own two-year-old daughter, still drowsy from nap time, curled up on my lap. I stroked her hair softly, sang sweet lullabies, and eventually, when she was ready to face the world, she got up.

"I, too, had dishes and laundry to do, errands to run, and a baby to feed. But my memories of childhood tugged at my heart. I was so happy with myself that I had allowed my need for perfection to slip for a while. Only then did I realize how my own mother managed that special lap time. She, too, had allowed chores to wait.

"I also realized my mother had given me two precious gifts, one to her daughter the child, the other to her daughter the adult. To the child, she gave comfort, love, security, and intimacy. To the adult, she modeled a valuable lesson: that a mother's lap is a child's sanctuary.

"Thanks, Mom; I needed both."

Carla Risener Bresnahan, <u>Welcome Home</u> magazine, May 1993

From the moment my first daughter arrived at five o'clock one December morning, with her wispy blond hair and blue-green eyes, she captivated me. A graduate student in literature at the time, I suddenly discovered that Huck Finn and the American novel couldn't begin to compete with the wonder and totality of motherhood. And Holly made me a mother. Not only did she expand my world and change my identity then, but she has been pushing and prodding me ever since to see the world in a more expansive way. How does she do this? By simply being herself.

Instead of going to a well-heeled suburban church like her parents, Holly has chosen to embrace a struggling city church with a heart for the poor. And when she feels I'm too steeped in psychological jargon, she waves mind-expanding novels in my face. While in college her months of blue and red hair and her secondhand rags gave me heartburn. But as I watch Holly live her life today, I am proud that this wonderful woman with a compassionate heart and firm convictions is my daughter. She's a woman I admire, a young woman I enjoy. Over the years we've become more than mother and daughter. Now we're friends. Colleagues. Partners in fun.

—*Brenda*

This past fall I watched my friend Eleanor care for her fragile eighty-seven-year-old mother as she lay dying. Ilde had several, rapidly growing brain tumors and gradually faded into unconsciousness on her last day as she lay in a hospital bed in her son-in-law's study, surrounded by cards and photos from family and friends.

A resilient woman who had continued to drive her own car, taking solo trips up and down the East Coast, Ilde had gone on a hayride with her grandchildren in her early eighties, and savored her cigarettes until she found out she had lung cancer at eighty-five. She was hardly the kind of woman to "go gently into that good night." After all, earlier in her life she had fought cancer four times and won. So when her doctor told her she could buy time—precious family time—if she elected to have brain surgery, she wagered and lost. Instead of months of clarity, she had only days. During their mother's brief periods of clarity followed by deepening unresponsiveness, Eleanor and her sister Anne faithfully nursed Ilde around the clock, with only occasional relief from a hospice nurse.

Whenever I visited Eleanor and Ilde during this time, I watched my friend care for her mother with great tenderness and devotion. No nurse, Eleanor fed her mother, whose brain no longer told her to swallow, through a tube inserted into her abdomen, an opening Eleanor carefully swabbed several times a day. And through the night my friend listened to her mother's restless sounds via a baby monitor, often emerging from her own bedroom bleary-eyed the next morning.

When I told Eleanor that she needed to get out of her house to take frequent little breaks, she replied, "But I *want* to do this. Mom doesn't have much time left. Besides—and you may not understand this—caring for her is a blessing." So care for her she did, often gently wiping her mother's forehead as she lay sleeping. And when it became apparent that the end was near, Anne put a newspaper under her mother's hands and carefully painted her nails. "She always took care of herself. She was meticulous about her appearance," said Anne with her eyes moist. "I know mom would want her nails to look good for the viewing."

Anne and Eleanor did not have a perfect relationship with their mother. Nor did they always have a peaceful one. Bright, strong-minded, the acknowledged matriarch of her family, Ilde occasionally tried to dominate her daughters' lives. On occasion their houses rang with noisy arguments as each daughter worked to establish her separate identity. But these three women loved each other fiercely and with great tenacity. Each was intensely loyal to the others. And underneath any anger flowed a river of love and positive regard. "It was stormy at times," acknowledged Anne, "but what close relationship isn't?"

The day Ilde died, she was surrounded by women who cared for her deeply: her two daughters and twin sisters. As she grew increasingly unresponsive, the four sang hymns, Eleanor read from the Bible, and she and Anne prayed. But even as Ilde faced the end, she struggled to cooperate with her daughters. All day long her heart raced like a marathon runner's while Anne frantically attempted to close her mother's bank account. Ilde even struggled to put an X on a necessary document. And only after her son Victor called did she stop racing toward the end. "You can let go now, Mom," he said. "Your affairs are in order. We love you. You can let go." An hour later Ilde died. And as the four kept their vigil, they discovered as one of Ilde's sisters said, "that death is the holiest of moments." And so it was and is.

Sometimes praying her mother into eternity is a daughter's final gift to the woman who bore her and over the years became her dearest and oldest friend.

—Brenda

Sisters: A Special Kind of Double

"Nobody's seen the trouble I've seen but you."

A D R I E N N E   R I C H ,   <u>L E A F L E T S</u>

For as long as I can remember, my sister, Sandy, has been an integral part of my life. This may seem strange since we grew up in different cities. Because of our father's untimely death when I was a toddler and Sandy was a baby, our mother chose to leave Sandy at our paternal grandparents' home and take me with her to a nearby mountain town where she worked as a telephone operator. As a result, Sandy grew up on a sprawling North Carolina dairy farm with Granny and Granddaddy, while I lived in various apartments with my nomadic mother. Only on holidays were we together. Then we were no longer lonely, only children but were united. True-blue sisters. My sister remembers that when I came it was as if a "fairy princess" had arrived. While I never felt like a princess, each Christmas and every summer vacation when I boarded a bus for the farm, I knew I was going to the most stable, secure place in my childhood. At the end of my hour-long journey, I would see Sandy standing at the bus stop, holding Granddaddy's hand.

Those vacations spent on the farm were the halcyon days of my childhood. Sandy and I roamed the farm, catching June bugs, picking blackberries, chasing downy baby ducks and chickens. Some days Sandy and I tiptoed into our aunt Faye's room, which was definitely off-limits. While she worked in town, we tried on her bras over our tee shirts and devoured her stacks of movie magazines, feeling like marauders. And as we grew, we became each other's cheerleader, protector, friend.

When Sandy fell behind in memorizing the multiplication tables, incurring Granddaddy's criticism, I intervened and tutored her until she could recite them by heart. Later when I needed to earn money for majorette camp, she and I spent a hot week in early August, trudging down dusty country roads, selling newspaper subscriptions door-to-door. Unselfishly, Sandy gave all her earnings to me. Recently as we were reflecting on our childhood, Sandy said, "We not only parented each other; we supported one another's dreams."

This past year, as we cared for our mother during her six hospitalizations, we were forced to confront unresolved tensions between us. Growing up as only children gave each of us a different legacy, and it has been hard to sort out the conflicting emotions. After we had a particularly loud and angry argument over the telephone, Sandy drove to a mountain retreat to speak to hundreds of women about God's love and forgiveness. As she prayed all the way up the mountain, an inner voice said gently, "I want you and Brenda to have peace between you." From that rocky time, God has taken us on a yearlong journey of healing and repair. As we have cared for our mother, we have reworked the past, talking, laughing, crying together. Something inside each of us has gone quiet. More careful of each other's feelings now than ever before, we call each other often and chat as friends. And in dealing with our negative feelings, we have recovered the love that was always there, buried though it was for a season. It feels good to have a true-blue sister again, to feel proud of her accomplishments, and to admire the woman she's become.

—*Brenda*

"I survived the death of our parents, but I can't imagine surviving without my sister. I wouldn't want to be alive without her."

—*Michelle D'Ambrosio, as quoted in* <u>Sisters</u>

When sisters are close, they can give each other something often lacking in other female friendships—practical help. You look to your sister for advice, emotional support, and help with the day-to-day demands of living—especially if you're married and your husband is not very involved in child rearing. It's important to have someone to pinch-hit as a baby-sitter, bring you soup when your family is felled by the flu, and look after you with all the tenderness and tenacity of a golden retriever.

"I'm very lucky. I don't have a husband, but I do have a sister. A sister I can talk to about personal things I wouldn't tell anyone else. A sister who does things for me, consoles me, comforts me. A sister with whom I can share my burdens and my joys. It's very hard in this world to find someone who can walk in your shoes, but you come closer than anybody. A lot of sisters are not friends. You, Edythe, like Maya Angelou has said, are my sister-friend."

—*Coretta Scott King,*
as quoted in <u>Sisters</u>

Sisterhood conjures up a welter of complex emotions. On a bad day, you envision your sister as the offspring of Genghis Khan and Mother Teresa. Or Cindy Crawford and the traitor Aldrich Ames. In the sister state, the emotional thermometer ricochets between love and hate. Who else can make you so angry? Who else can be so compassionate?

"She was my protector, my lookout, my voice at the drugstore counter when I was too shy to ask for help. She killed the spiders, led the way home, rang doorbells for trick or treat. She grew up bold, with a secret shyness. I grew up shy, with a secret boldness. I was sixteen when she left for college. I still remember the grief I felt....

"Our mother died when we were twenty-one and twenty-three. We eyed each other hopefully for signs that we could fill the awful gap for each other. We couldn't. We were sisters, comrades, competitors, peers. We had nurtured our strengths in each other's full view: that left little hope of magic. But we knew we had come from the same woman, and we knew we'd been gypped in the same way.

"Sisterhood is to friendship what an arranged marriage is to romance. You are thrown together for life, no questions asked (until later), no chance of escape. And if you're lucky, you find love despite the confinement."

—*Lisa Grunwald, novelist, <u>Glamour</u>, July 1995*

What helps sisters forge an enduring friendship? Their relationship with their mother is key. "My mother taught us to be close," says Jennifer, a pretty brunette and mother of two boys. "I remember the first birthday party I attended when I was six. Julie, then four, wasn't invited, and I can still see her unhappy little face pressed against the window as she waved good-bye. My mother handled the situation beautifully. She not only told me to bring a special surprise back for Julie, but she said to Julie, 'I know you feel sad, but each of you needs to have your own set of friends.' My mother helped us see each other as separate people."

Over the years Jennifer's mom patiently instructed both girls in the art of sisterhood. "She taught each of us to be the other's cheerleader," said Jennifer. "When I got an award, my mother taught Julie to be happy for me because her time would come. And it did."

"Even in the most patriarchal of families, mother is *the* most important person in determining how sisters relate to each other. Whether the sisters number two or eight, mother is central to their dynamics. Whether mother dies in childbirth or outlives her daughters, she is omnipresent. Whether mother was loving or emotionally absent, she leaves her lasting impression on her daughters, individually and together—for mother is the role model of the sisters' feminine identity."

—Barbara Mathias, *Between Sisters*

"My sister is four years older. As kids, I was her Barbie doll. She told me outrageous stories, and I believed everything. We shared a room. One night I woke up, and she said she had just been taken away by aliens. 'Didn't you know? Everybody has a special time. They come and get you.' I was so excited. I waited and waited, but the aliens never came.

"She also told me Olivia Newton John and Elton John were sister and brother. Then one day I found out from the most disgusting boy in class that they weren't. I was horrified. I couldn't believe my sister would blatantly lie to me. But she did. Without remorse, even. At that moment cynicism entered my life."

—Monica, 31, a policy director

"Of the many relationships in a woman's life, the bond between sisters is unique, stretching and bending through periods of closeness and distance, but almost never breaking. Sisterly ties tend to have fewer emotional knots than the ones that bind mothers and daughters. Sisters are girlfriends, rivals, listening posts, shopping buddies, confidantes and so much more.

"Research shows that women who have strong connections with their sisters are less likely to be depressed. In one study, women said they felt the world was a safer place because they had sisters to depend upon in times of crisis.... Sisters function as a safety net in a chaotic world simply by being there for each other."

—Carol Saline and Sharon J. Wohlmuth, Sisters

My Sister, the Queen

"My sister and I have been entangled from the womb, but not because we shared it at the same time. She occupied it first. Ever since, the message has been clear: first come, first served. This message was summarized well in a birthday card she recently gave me: 'Happy Birthday to my Sister the Princess,' it says on the outside. On the inside: 'From her Sister the Queen.'

"Sandy and I grew from the same bone house, from the same mother's soul. Maybe that's why it gets so confusing. Hers was one of the first faces looming over my crib, and she stuck more than fingers in between the bars, poking, probing, reminding me that I would never outshine her, never have a shadow as large as hers. Her goal, it seemed, was to keep me measuring just how large that shadow was.

"Once when I was about eleven years old and triumphantly mowing the half-acre front yard with a hand mower, Sandy arrived on the scene. I said rather proudly, 'Look, I did this all by myself. I'm almost finished.' Four years older than I, she said: 'Can I just push the mower a little bit?' 'Okay,' I said.

"She struggled with the twirling metal beast no more than six feet, turned to me, unclutched the handle, and slapped her hands together. Just before running off she announced, 'Now you can't say you did it all by yourself.'

"Of course there were other times, some funny, some not, humiliation being the modus operandi. When I wanted an old purse of hers, she demanded, 'Only if you kiss my feet.' Barefoot, her feet neither smelled nor looked so good. Reptilian is the closest adjective I can come up with. Being an animal lover, however, I suffered the agony of bending to her feet, only to have her change her mind.

"We got older. I grew breasts larger and sooner than she. That pretty much finished us. Jealousy raged, although I didn't understand this until I became an adult. Now as a thirty-eight-year-old woman I've come to believe sisters are born with an innate competitiveness that both drives and melds us simultaneously. Our relationship is fraught with conflict, but beneath the prize of mother, father and siblings, beyond measuring the shadow, there's something deeper. Something that's taken me decades to grasp. She's my best friend.

"At forty-two, Sandy insists we are twins when we meet strangers or when I am introduced to her friends. I squirm; she beams. The truth is we do look alike, but can't they see all those wrinkles around her eyes? The less defined jaw line? I claim I am younger and laugh. I say, 'I'm the newer, improved version.' She gets red, mad, silent. She's never admitted she's been wrong, at least when it comes to me.

"As adults, there's no one like a sister to remind you of who you once were, what your foibles are, what history you hail from, and most of all, what mistakes and sins you've committed. But my sister's there, a few houses away from me. Maybe if we lived a few states apart, the relationship might be less intense. No matter what the distance, I know she's there; we can't escape each other. We don't want to.

"Underlying our history from the womb, a belief in each other surfaces despite the conflicts. There's little more powerful than that belief. She knows who I am. She's been there since my beginning. She'll always be there. We share a language only families understand: a heart kind of Braille. Touching, knowing, supporting.

"I've come to understand that in my sister's shadow there is shade for me. In her, I've found a lifetime companion."

—*Sherry Karasik, freelance journalist*

My sister and I have been through many phases in our relationship. As a child, I was her idol. While she still rode a tiny red tricycle, I had graduated to a pink bike with training wheels and sailed ahead as she furiously pedaled—chubby baby legs flying—yelling, "Wait for me. Wait for me!"

It wasn't until high school that I became persona non grata. As a senior, I hung out with track team friends while my sister befriended the more popular football and cheerleading set. Later, when we ended up at the same college, I was beyond her ability to understand, as I served up pots of bean goo, hung out with the pretentious literati, and donned the proverbial black of an intellectual aspirant.

Luckily, her marriage has brought her back to me. Now we are the best of friends and talk nearly every day. Living a block away has been a real gift; our respective apartments are outposts for adventure. We've had many spontaneous dinners, afternoon teas, or just plain powwows. During the blizzard of '96 when snow blanketed Washington, D.C. and immobilized its denizens, we shoveled out our driveways with pails and dustpans and headed to the video store to enjoy a multipack evening. Many are the Sunday afternoons when I'll get a call. "What are you doing?" says a voice that's two-thirds guileless six-year-old, one-third temptress. That's code for "Can I come over?" And she does. Together we while away pleasant hours, sharing our souls over Cokes, spreadable cheese and crackers, and chocolate. We trust each other not to divulge the things that hurt.

It's easy, as her husband knows, to see she's beautiful through and through. What's amazing is that it took me this long to realize it. Could my wonderful new friend be the same fluffy-haired urchin who used to pinch me into screams on unending car trips?

—Holly

"My sister is my best, best friend," says Melanie, a Washingtonian, about her Oklahoma-based only sister. "She knows every detail of my life; there are no secrets. She's supportive no matter what. She's also someone I play with. We've gone on cruises together, flown to Florida, and taken day trips all around our respective states.

"We have a tenacious bond; we help each other see the grass is greener than we think it is as we share the joys and frustrations of being single."

—Melanie, 31, a sales executive

"Brothers share the biological link, but they're…well…just different. They rarely seem as emotionally glued as girls who grew up under the same roof. What sets sisters apart from brothers—and also from friends—is a very intimate meshing of heart, soul and the mystical cords of memory."

—*Carol Saline and Sharon J. Wohlmuth, Sisters*

If we can't be close to our sisters because of physical or emotional distance, then we need to turn our friends into sisters. Friend-sisters can become as intimate as family; while not bound to them by blood, we are nonetheless tied to each other by love and mutual regard. As surrogate family, our closest friends are there for us, attending life's important celebrations, extending practical help, and listening to our hearts.

Research shows that friendship between sisters ebbs and flows across the life cycle. Sisters are most often close as children, more distant as young adults, but close again as they mature and move into midlife and beyond.

—*Adapted from Toni A. H. McNaron, The Sister Bond*

When a client comes to my office and says she wants to better understand her mother, I send her to her mother's sister. Her aunt, as a family historian, has invaluable information in her memory bank, information that can help my client see her mother as a flesh-and-blood being. If the sister is perceptive or insightful, she can talk about the mother's emotional connections to their mother, father, friends, and herself. And as my client learns about her mother— through the eyes of a sister—I see her gradually change. Not only does she begin to understand her mother in greater richness and depth, but she taps into her own psychological roots. And it sometimes happens that she and her mother begin to have a more open, honest relationship, aided in great measure by the understanding she has gleaned from her mother's sister.

—Brenda

"A sister can be seen as someone who is both ourselves and very much not ourselves—a special kind of double."

—Toni A. H. McNaron, The Sister Bond

Our sisters never cease to be important to us. As part of our first family, they share our genetic legacy, complete our personalities, finish our sentences, share our hotel beds, fork food off our plates, and generally make themselves at home in our company, whether we are in Paris or Pittsburgh. For *home* is what they will always represent to us. It's bundled up in their being. And if we can remain close throughout our lives, they will add technicolor and stereo sound to the movie of our lives.

—Holly

Mentors and Pathfinders

"You never know when someone may catch a dream from you."

H E L E N   L O W R I E   M A R S H A L L

Mentoring has a long history. In fact, one of the loveliest passages in all of literature is on this subject. It describes a relationship between two women—one younger, the other, older. These women were not sisters, mothers, daughters, or even childhood friends. Although related by marriage, they were bound together by something much deeper than blood ties. The younger woman loved the older woman deeply. She told her:

> Entreat me not to leave you,
>> or to turn back from following after you;
> for wherever you go, I will go,
>> and wherever you lodge, I will lodge;
> your people shall be my people,
>> and your God, my God.

—Ruth 1:16, NKJV

So said Ruth to her embittered mother-in-law, Naomi. Saddened by the loss of her husband and two sons, Naomi faced an uncertain and poverty-stricken future. Or so she thought. "Leave me," she told her two daughters-in-law. Orpah did, but not Ruth. She stayed and in so doing became the consummate example of loyalty, commitment, and obedience to a mothering figure she loved dearly.

As the story unfolds, we see that God honored Ruth's devotion. Because of Naomi, Ruth met her future husband, Boaz. And because of Ruth, Naomi had economic provision for her old age, status, the position of wise woman at the city gate, and a grandson Obed, who would become the grandfather of David, king of the Israelites.

Webster's defines a mentor as a "trusted counselor and guide," but she is much more. She may be a pathfinder who is ten to twenty years older, or she may be a peer who has scaled the mountain we intend to climb. She calls down from farther up the mountain and says, "Come on up. The view is wonderful here. Watch the rocks, stay on the path, and you'll make it up safely." As a guide, this pathfinder sharpens our skills, enlarges our perceptions, and gives us the confidence that, like her, we can overcome obstacles and achieve our dreams.

"When I was in telecommunications sales, Denise and I were the only women in our department. She was promoted from a lower sales job to a higher one. Our boss was really harsh, and Denise was nice and meek. I thought, 'I've got to help this girl or she'll get eaten alive.' So I showed her the ropes, and she prayed me into the kingdom."

—Sylvia, 35, a telecommunications consultant

When I asked the women in the workplace whether they had ever had female mentors, I got a lot of blank stares. The common response was "Women don't help other women." That's a sad commentary on modern times. Men have been helping other men for decades; it's called the "Old Boys Network." Why can't we form a group of our own? We could call it Corporate Climbing Chicks. Collegiality isn't a sin; it's a necessity. Let's help each other, whether we're three months or thirty years ahead. We may even make new friends in the process.

—Holly

"My commitment to mentoring came from my early years as a young professional. Many offered criticism. Few offered help. I vowed if I survived I would help others in their spiritual and professional journeys."

—Dr. Patricia Ennis,
college professor

Once when I spoke to a group of young mothers in Seattle, Washington, a young woman walked up, holding the hand of her blond, cherubic, three-year-old daughter. Wearily she said, "I have tried to find an older woman to become involved in my life, and I have talked to many leaders in this church. But to date I haven't found anyone. Where are all those Titus Two moms who are supposed to nurture us and help us become better wives and mothers?"

If I saw this young woman today, I'd tell her to place an ad in the church bulletin that read: "Wanted: An older woman who has loved being a mom and wants to share what she's learned in the trenches with a new recruit. Tidy house not necessary, perfect children not expected. An open spirit, a desire to befriend a younger woman, and a willingness to grow are the only position requirements."

—Brenda

In an earlier era, cross-generational friendships were celebrated and expected. Young women—especially young mothers—could call a friend from church, a next-door neighbor, a relative, a kindly acquaintance for help in navigating the sometimes turbulent river of parenting. Today, few women have nourishing cross-generational friendships. As a result, some find the boot camp of mothering a bewildering experience. And many are starving for friendships with older women. Said a thirty-year-old, "I long for a woman to come alongside, put her arm around me, and say, 'You can do it.'"

A mentor is a friend for all seasons: adolescence, singleness, marriage, motherhood, menopause, even old age. She helps us open and close the important chapters in our lives.

In my self-appointed role as mentor-maker, I try to say to women my age and older who are reluctant to take on a younger charge, "Wait a minute. You're missing out on so much fun. Let me tell you about the joy I've had touching younger women's lives." And I show them treasured letters I've received from readers of my books over the years and the pictures of moms and babies scattered around the house. I tell them about the three younger women who have deepened my spirituality and enriched my life as I've opened my heart to them.

Then I don my psychologist hat and tell women that the research shows we will be happier in midlife if we're nurturing the younger generation. As the late Harvard psychoanalyst Erik Erikson said, the task of midlife is "generativity"—"guiding the next generation." And if we are too much lost in bridge, career, or our own family to reach out, we just may shuffle into old age with regret. Not only does psychology tell us to pass the torch, but Scripture mandates it.

So we have no excuse for closing our hearts to younger women. And though our lifestyles may have changed over the past thirty years, our emotional needs as women have remained the same. All of us need someone to guide, encourage, and love us. And for a young woman, that someone is an older woman rich in life experience and wisdom who can help her define and shape her life.

—Brenda

"Likewise, teach the older women to be reverent in the way they live...but to teach what is good. Then they can train the younger women to love their husbands and children, to be self-controlled and pure, to be busy at home, to be kind, and to be subject to their husbands, so that no one will malign the word of God."

Titus 2:3—5

As female professionals, we need to seek out mentors who will help us advance through the ranks. Women need to find mentors who are "higher ranking, influential, senior organization members with advanced experience and knowledge who are committed to providing upward mobility and support to a protégé's professional career," says Belle Rose Ragins. Mentors usually sign on for the long-term, filter inside information to their protégés, and act as a buffer between the organization and the individual. By providing guidance and support, mentors help develop their protégés' self-confidence. With all these benefits, one would think that most women would be scrambling to find senior colleagues to help them. Not so. According to one study, less than 20 percent of women surveyed were looking for a mentor.

—Adapted from Belle Rose Ragins,
"Barriers to Mentoring,"
Human Relations

A Catholic priest once said that throughout his life, at stressful or important moments, someone invariably came along and extended a hand. He gratefully took the hand and walked with that person for a season, feeling comforted and stretched as a human being, growing deeper in his faith in God. Isn't that what a mentor does—extends a hand and walks with us for a time?

A woman from Tucson, Arizona, said of her mentor, "The ugliest parts of me were exposed, accepted and relabeled with positive words. At times I ran from her, yet felt drawn to her because she helped me see that I neither had to be perfect or positive. Only real."

—Adapted from Virtue magazine, June 1993

Being a young woman in the nineties is a tremendous challenge. The single life can be a hard one. Women are supposed to maintain drop-dead looks and the figure of an Olympic pentathlete while working long hours at amazing careers. What's the reality? For many of us, confusion. It's hard to wed personal and societal expectations, to persevere on the Christian walk, to keep our focus, to continue to hope and not be weighed down by disappointments. And it's a great relief when women—five, ten, twenty years down the path of womanhood—stop to offer advice, help, career direction, a vision for the future. I value advice from working women, career moms, at-home mothers. The married and single alike.

My peers and I aren't as independent as we look; in many cases we have no choice but to skipper our little sailboats into choppy seas. It helps if friendly ports are nearby.

—*Holly*

She Gave the Softest Hugs

"It's a cool morning in May, and as I clean up the kitchen, I'm looking forward to working in the garden and yard. Taking off my apron, I fondly remember my mother-in-law, Phyllis, who gave me this purple and green apron because it no longer fit her.

"The apron has recently taken on a special meaning; it brings back memories. If one image comes to mind, it's of Phyllis waiting for us to arrive from out of town. Wearing a housecoat, slippers, and a long apron hanging from her shoulders to her knees, she would invite us into her warm kitchen. I never thought of her as being the 'old fatty' she often called herself with self-deprecating humor. Rather, she exemplified all the traits of the quintessential grandma. Phyllis was caring and giving and had an aura of peaceful serenity.

"My younger daughter summed it up well when she once said, 'Grandma gives the softest hugs!' Even in her later years, I could still see the beauty in her strong Greek features of wavy black hair, the smoothest creamy skin, and big brown eyes.

"I can still hear her calling 'Hi, Paaaam!' from inside the house. And we'd hug and kiss. We'd sit at the kitchen table, she and I, and we'd talk about the latest family news. She'd reach out and tap me on the arm to make a point, her affectionate way of emphasizing something.

"While we were quite different, the warmth of home and family life was our common bond. In addition, we both loved to have a good laugh, and we both liked the color purple—we often would exchange purple items for gifts.

"Though we were often separated by several states, we managed to keep in touch by writing letters to each other. She always addressed them just to me. They came often enough that I began to expect them, and I could almost predict their arrival.

"Early on in my marriage, Phyllis said I could call her Mom. Having married so young (at twenty-one) and having a loving and close relationship with my own mother, I couldn't imagine calling another woman 'Mom.' But I was quick to tell my new mother-in-law that it didn't mean I loved her any less. She never mentioned it again, and I think I proved to her over the fifteen years I knew her how genuine my feelings were. We got along quite well and began to be good pen pals. I'd write newsy letters filled with details of all our activities. Phyllis would write back, telling me how much she loved reading my letters or how she laughed as she read about the antics of her grandchildren.

"Phyllis never finished high school but kept the family budget perfectly balanced; she and her husband Andrew put three kids through college on a steelworker's paycheck. She instilled in her children tremendous values, as well as a deep respect for themselves and others.

"It was May 1990, and Phyllis and Andrew were due for a visit. So several of us went shopping and bought pretty lavender and green scented candles and soaps and baskets, a few things we knew Grandma would like. As usual, they were scheduled to arrive from West Virginia around lunch time on Friday. But instead of a knock at the door, the phone rang, and a voice said, 'Mrs. Goresh? I'm calling from the Hagerstown Hospital. Your father-in-law is fine, but your mother-in-law became ill on the trip. She has died of a heart attack.'

"Hours later I sat alone in the living room. What could I say? What could I do?

"Andy drove to Hagerstown to meet his father. When Andy and his dad returned, words stuck in my throat, and tears spilled from my eyes to see Andrew walk in alone. With red-rimmed eyes, Andrew hugged me and said, 'Phyllis was so happy this morning. She was looking forward to celebrating Samantha's birthday.'

"When I talked with Phyllis's sister, Mary, about funeral arrangements, Mary mentioned that Phyllis had always loved the color pink. 'Phyllis should be laid to rest in a pink dress,' she said. How about that? All those years she'd let me think her favorite color was purple so we would have something in common.

"As I passed her casket, I picked up a pink flower, paused, and thought, 'No, Phyllis and I shared purple.' I put the pink flower down and reached instead for a lovely lavender iris and gave it to her."

Pam Goresh, <u>Welcome Home</u> magazine, May 1993

chapter 7

Making Friends with the Other Sex

*"Husbands were made to be talked to. It helps them
concentrate their minds on what they're reading."*

C. S. LEWIS

Why Men Aren't Enough—
the Man's Explanation

"According to a recent scientific study, conducted while I had a cup of coffee at Borders bookstore, women are approximately 473 times more likely to spend money on 'who am I and how did I get this way?' books than men are. In fact, on any given day when the Gothic romance section is overcrowded, this ratio expands to 642 to 1.

"As part of my scientific research, I visited the 'who am I and how did I get this way?' section one day, taking the understandable precautions of donning an Alan Alda disguise and tucking a well-worn, tear-stained copy of *The Bridges of Madison County* under my arm. Astounding sight: shelf after shelf of books about women and their mothers, women and their sisters, women and their second cousins once-removed. On another shelf—women and pain, women and misery, women and love, women in pain in love, women in love with pain. A section on women and their bodies: love your body (ages twenty to thirty), learning to live with your body (ages thirty to forty), how to ignore your body (post-forty).

"Men don't read these kinds of books for a very good reason: the basic question 'who am I and how did I get this way?' just doesn't interest us because we already know who we are, we're late for work, and we don't have time to think about it.

"Chances are, if the book jacket doesn't have a picture of a tool on the cover, we aren't going to mess with it.

"Nevertheless, all married men have sincerely wrestled with the second most important question that troubles women, to wit, 'Why doesn't my husband meet all my needs?' In fact, most of us wrestle with this question every night in bed because at the precise moment we are dropping off to sleep our wives gently remind us in their loving, sensitive, nurturing way that we sure aren't getting the job done in the 'true intimacy' department.

"After years of scientific research, I am pleased to report that men have now discovered the answer to this question. Unassailable evidence has been amassed to support the view among men that women are indeed from another planet. For example, women dress to meet the approval of other women, not to impress men. No man, of course, dresses to please another man.

"Women talk about things as a means of finding out what they think; men think issues through before they speak in order to say exactly what they mean. Women talk about problems and conflicts in order to sort out their feelings— 'How did that make you feel, dear?' Men assess the situation and offer a solution. Men want to know 'What did you do?'

"Men build; women make nests.

"Men buy stuff; women shop.

"Men have buddies; women need true friends.

"These differences are clearly the result of different planetary origins. So, it is no surprise that women seek out their own kind to have many of their basic emotional needs met. (The well-adjusted man accepts this situation. He relishes it. He wishes she would stop asking so many questions and just go see her friends.)

"So, when a male-female conflict arises, the male can reassure himself by remembering, 'She's from another planet.' You, of course, will be thinking, 'Men are so shallow. I'm glad that women are deep. We're superior.'

"Herein lies the basis for true contentedness."

—Scott McMichael, lieutenant colonel in the army

My husband, Don, has learned to monitor my best friend's travel schedule. When she goes out of town, he knows he will feel greater pressure to be intimate. His innocent query, "How was your day?" becomes a journey into the inner reaches of my personality. Then if I probe his psyche, he says he feels like an insect under a magnifying lens. "When is Ells coming back?" he moans after an intense evening of eyeball-to-eyeball communication where I haven't blinked once. "Soon," I reassure him. The next night Ells, who's on grandmother duty in Kansas City, calls. And as I saunter toward the phone, I hear a sign of relief from the family room as my husband paws underneath sofa cushions for a buried remote control, flips through TV channels, and settles with a squeak into his favorite green easy chair. Enough "real" communication; it's time for football!

—Brenda

Forget David and Jonathan, Achilles and Patroclus, Butch Cassidy and the Sundance Kid! In research conducted by psychologist Joel Block, 84 percent of the men studied said they would not dare open up to other men. Block writes, "Upon being interviewed about their comrades, men frequently spoke of distrust and only occasionally of loyalty. Having learned caution, they expected neither sympathy nor devotion from their brothers. On the contrary, their experiences are filled with incidents of rivalry and betrayal."

So what do men do when they want to speak from the heart? They turn to those they feel they can trust—they, along with women themselves, find a woman to talk to. Women, then, are the intimacy experts for both sexes.

—Adapted from Joel Block,

Friendship: How to Give It, How to Get It

"The average man's idea of an intimate exchange is the average woman's idea of a casual conversation."

—Letty Pogbrebin, Among Friends

When I lost a best friend six years ago, I ran to the one person I felt would understand—my husband, Don. One afternoon when I was feeling low, Don left work early to meet me at a coffee shop. Astute man that he is, he had seen the rupture coming and knew how much I had invested in this important friendship. As I looked toward the door, I saw Don walk in, carrying a long, white florist's box. "Here," he said smiling, "I know how much she meant to you, and this is a token of my love." Inside were a dozen, long-stemmed, red roses.

—Brenda

Women approach the conversational world as an individual in a network of connections. In this world, conversations are a way to connect and to show empathy and concern, to give confirmation and support, to reach consensus. Men, on the other hand, see conversations as negotiations in which they try to achieve and maintain the upper hand. For men, talk is information, and life is a contest, a struggle to preserve independence and avoid failure. "From childhood, men learn to use talking as a way to get and keep attention," says Deborah Tannen, linguistics professor at Georgetown University. She believes that men are more comfortable speaking publicly to strangers than privately to the loves of their lives.

—Adapted from Deborah Tannen, You Just Don't Understand

Men sometimes have to take refuge from the women in their lives; they find sanctuary and understanding in the company of other men. One man, the father of two adolescent daughters and husband of a middle-aged wife with raging hormones, told friends ruefully, "At our house there's never a good week." He finally found relief when he joined an underground survivors group, a semisecret weekly gathering with four buddies at a local diner. What are they surviving? Their wives' menopause, of course.

My friend John is the brother I never had. Our friendship is at once fierce and friendly, our genuine affection for each other only occasionally scarred by hotly contested games of Liverpool and jogging sessions that evolve into breakneck bolts to the finish line. With John, I can be myself: silly, loud, competitive, whiny. He responds in kind with louder whines or more childish behavior, as a big brother would. And as I watch him interact tenderly with his wife, Lisa—also a cherished friend—I absorb important lessons about life and love, lessons I hope to transfer to a marriage of my own one day. After a few ill-fated stabs at romance, it's encouraging and healing to see a man who truly loves his wife and lives his beliefs. It's important to round out our female friendships with significant male ones—to allow men to be our friends, role models, brothers, and competitors at fun. Otherwise, we miss more than we know.

—Holly

"Women have a capacity for communication that men just don't have. Sometimes a woman can communicate to another woman, 'You're not crazy' while a man may be thinking, 'This *is* crazy.' A woman bonds with another woman in ways men can't, but I think this is part of God's plan. You know, He didn't just create marriage. He created society. A woman alone is not a good thing. A woman with a man is better, but still incomplete. So husbands should encourage their wives to have friends. I have prayed for Susan to have friends throughout our marriage. In fact, I see my wife's friends as coworkers in helping her be fulfilled."

—John Yates, pastor and author

"Being true friends with women is, in a way, the path of least resistance, but being close friends with the men in our lives is more challenging. Throughout our lives we need to listen to both male and female voices."

—Charmaine Yoest,
author, wife, and mother of two

The Father of All Comfort

"There is only one way to love God:
to take not a single step without him, and to follow
with a brave heart wherever he leads."

FRANÇOIS FÉNELON

od will, if we allow it, become the closest friend we've ever known. Once we know in our hearts that He is *with* us and *for* us, we cease to feel so bereft or alone. He is closer than a whisper, more comforting than a good mother.

I discovered this a quarter of a century ago when my first husband, a psychiatric resident at Yale, left in pursuit of a new love. Many nights I grieved the death of my young marriage and David's betrayal. Face down upon the carpet or staring out into the night sky, I called to God. And He came. Inside my heart I heard these words:

"Do not be afraid; you will not suffer shame.

Do not fear disgrace; you will not be humiliated....

The LORD will call you back

as if you were a wife deserted and distressed in spirit—

a wife who married young,

only to be rejected," says your God.

"For a brief moment I abandoned you,

but with deep compassion I will bring you back....

I will have compassion on you,"

says the LORD your Redeemer.

—Isaiah 54:4, 6–8

And so it has been across the years. During those painful days and long nights, I discovered that friendship with God needs to be the foundation of all our other human connections. How else will they ever work? And if we have never made His acquaintance? Or if, knowing Him, we neglect this crucial and life-giving friendship? Then we will live a half-life in the here and now and have no assurance of eternity. He alone puts eternity in our hearts and gives us traveling companions for the journey there.

—*Brenda*

"In reality, a few years difference in the dates of our birth, a few more miles between certain houses, the choice of one university instead of another, posting to different regiments, the accident of a topic being raised at a first meeting—any of these chances might have kept us apart. But, for a Christian, there are, strictly speaking, no chances. A secret master of ceremonies has been at work."

—*C. S. Lewis, The Four Loves*

God alone is a friend for all seasons and for the sometimes lonely middle of the night hours when we can no longer in good conscience awaken a husband or decently dial a friend. In the blackness of night He soothes our fears, hears our longings, and assures us that we have "a future and a hope."

"It is amazing that a poor human creature is able to speak with God's high majesty in heaven and not be afraid. When we pray, the heart and the conscience must not pull away from God because of our sins and our unworthiness, or stand in doubt, or be scared away. When we pray we must hold fast and believe that God has heard our prayer. It was for this reason that the ancients defined prayer as an *Ascensus mentis ad Deum*, 'a climbing up of the heart unto God.'"

—*Martin Luther*

"Friends, our life is love and peace and tenderness. We are called to bear one another's burdens, forgive one another, and never judge or accuse one another. Instead, we must pray for one another, helping one another up with a tender hand if there has been any slip or fall. O! Wait to walk in this spirit that you may enjoy the Lord in sweetness and walk meekly, tenderly, peaceably, and lovingly with one another.... So watch your hearts and ways. Watch over one another in gentleness and tenderness. Know that we cannot help one another out of a snare in our own strength, for only the Lord, who must be waited upon can do this in all and for all."

—*Isaac Penington, British Quaker*

Though human—and limited by frailty and sin—Moses was called the friend of God. Of all God's special servants, Moses was so loved that "the Lord used to speak to Moses face to face, as one speaks to a friend." What greater praise can exist for anyone than to be called a friend of God? Too often we are content to be acquaintances of the most distant sort with our Lord and Father, when we could spend a lifetime deepening the most important friendship we will ever make.

"Eternal God, who so cares for every one of us as if thou carest for him alone, and so for all of us as if all were but one: Blessed is the man who loveth thee, and his friend in thee. And his enemy for thee. For he alone loses no one dear to him, to whom all are dear in Him who never can be lost."

—*St. Augustine*

"So if you want to find your true friends, I will tell you where to look. Begin with God. He is the only source of true and eternal friendship. You are best suited for spiritual communication and friendship when you sink into silence into the bosom of God. He means everything to the kind of friends you seek. They talk of him and live for him and their whole lives are wrapped up in him. That is why I tell you to sink into his bosom. That is where true friendship is."

—*François Fénelon,*
Christian philosopher

A Friend in a Far-Off Place

"I discovered what friendship means several years ago when I moved to Thailand, a strange and exotic country. I felt truly alone in ways that nobody seemed to understand. 'What a wonderful opportunity for you,' people said. 'Mmm, I know,' was my response. 'I wish I were going,' friends said. 'Be my guest,' I silently countered. Oh, I had promises of 'We'll keep in touch,' or 'We'll miss you!' but in reality it didn't ease those feelings of aloneness. 'Oh, God,' I prayed when I arrived, 'please send me some friends.' 'But I'm here,' He whispered. 'Yes, I know you are, but I need some friends.' 'Who am I?' He countered. I listened but still felt such anguish. He spoke, but I never really heard. I continued pleading with tears and a heavy heart. Then one day in prayer, I finally understood. I heard Him with my whole heart. He was the friend I longed for. First and foremost. I could go to Him with all my disappointments, fear, and vulnerability. He alone would never turn away, be unable to deal with my insecurities, or feel ill-equipped to advise and comfort me. With the Lord, I could be myself; I was accepted for all that was me. In time I began to feel nurtured and had absolute faith that whatever I did, however bad, I could always seek forgiveness; that wrong would be totally forgiven, never referred to, or held against me. This was the friendship I had been seeking all my life. This was the friendship I needed. When I finally internalized this, God sent me other friends. But however wonderful human friends are, I've learned that God is my first friend, for wherever I am, He is always with me."

—Maxine, foreign service administrator

Notes

Friends: Part Mother, Sister, Saint

1. Carin Rubenstein, "A 1993 New Woman Survey," *New Woman*, October 1993, 78.
2. Ibid., 81.
3. Ibid.
4. Ibid., 22.

Mothers and Daughters: First Friends

1. L. Alan Sroufe, "The Coherence of Individual Development," in *In the Beginning*, ed. Jay Belsky (New York: Columbia Press, 1982), 19.
2. Nancy Chodorow, *The Reproduction of Mothering* (Berkeley: University of California Press, 1978), 109.
3. Ruthellen Josselson, *Finding Herself: Pathways to Identity Development* (San Francisco: Jossey Bass, 1987), 171.

"A friend is a present you give yourself."

— ROBERT LOUIS STEVENSON